Finding God
in the Rest of the Story

Edmon L. Rowell, Jr.

PEAKE ROAD
Macon, Georgia

ISBN 1-57312-178-9

Finding God in the Rest of the Story

Edmon L. Rowell, Jr.

Copyright ©1998
Peake Road

Smyth & Helwys Publishing, Inc.
6316 Peake Road
Macon, Georgia 31210-3960
1-800-747-3016

The paper used in this publication meets the minimum
requirements of American National Standard for Information Sciences—
Permanence of Paper for Printed Library Materials, ANSI Z39.48–1984.

Library of Congress Cataloging-in-Publication Data

Rowell, Edd.
Finding God in the rest of the story / Edd Rowell.
    p.   cm.   Includes bibliographical references.
ISBN 1-57312-178-9 (alk. paper)
1. Meditations.
2. Baptists—Sermons.
3. Sermons, American.
I. Title.
BV4832.2R68 1998
252'.061—dc21

97-50025
CIP

Contents

For Ruth,
who, with regard to all that is best,
is the rest of the story of my life,

yet not only my life
but the lives of countless children,

our own,
and the hundreds of children,
many now with children of their own,
for whom
over the years
she has been and is

teacher,
caregiver,
guide,
helper,
friend.

For so many of us she really is
the rest of our story.

Foreword

"I don't know. You should probably call Edd!" More than once in my nine years as pastor of First Baptist Church in Macon, Georgia, I heard that pair of sentences: *"I don't know. You should probably call Edd."* Those words I heard more than once usually would be in response to an inquiry I had directed to one of the several outstanding theologians who serve at Mercer University. I would be seeking the long-lost source of some vague historical, literary, or theological allusion. Usually when I called for help, they could give me the answer. But occasionally, rarely, every now and then, they would not know. In those cases they would invariably say, *"I'm not sure . . . Better ask Edd."*

"Edd," in this case, functioned somewhat like "Elvis." There was no more need to say "Rowell" than there would be to say "Presley." I knew the Edd of whom they spoke, and we knew, they and I, that for the really tough cases of citing sources, tracking down authors, and verifying quotes, if Edd Rowell didn't know, it was exceedingly unlikely that anyone else would. More than once I have said to my wife, Marcia, "Of all the wonderfully intelligent people we know, I do believe that Edd is the most knowledgeable of the bunch." And it is so. When it comes to getting the facts, those who don't know where to go, but do know where to turn, call Edd.

But Edd knows something deeper, higher, and better than the facts. Edd's legendary knowledge of "the facts" is only part of the story. The rest of the story is that Edd knows the truth. And it is the truth that Edd tells us so clearly, simply, and honestly in the pages of this book. *Finding God in the Rest of the Story* is not about the facts Edd has gathered. It is about the truth Edd has learned, the truth he has learned from a lifetime of seeking God, following Jesus, studying Scripture, loving family, being a friend, and pastoring people. In these pages, Edd speaks from his quiet depths to our quiet depths. And what he has to say rings true "clear to the bone," as they say in Edd's native LA.

For those of us who know Edd Rowell, a book of his thoughts, stories, and sermons is long overdue. He has helped dozens of others to write and bind their words. It is past time for his own words to be written, bound, and offered to the wider light of a broader day. And thus, we rejoice to hold in our hands this book, a book written by a quiet, thoughtful soul who has been friend, editor, pastor, fact-finder, and truth-teller to so many for so long.

—Charles E. Poole

Looking for the Rest of the Story

And who knows the interpretation of a thing?
—Eccl 8:1 NRSV

Radio commentator Paul Harvey—who seems to have been around forever—has for years been looking for and telling the "rest of the story." So have I. It is often the "rest of the story" that explains and makes sense of the whole.

Since 1958, when I was pastor of and preacher to Steep Creek Baptist Church near Hope Hull, Alabama, I have been looking for the rest of the story in the hope of helping others (and myself) to find what we are all looking for.

Over the years I've wondered why Sunday after Sunday (Wednesdays too for us deep-dipt Baptists) and holy day after holy day, people keep on coming to church and keep on listening to the sermon.

People *really do listen.* I can see it in their hungry faces. I can hear it in their often pointed and perceptive remarks as they leave. People really listen. It is one reason why preaching is for me one of the most exhausting yet exhilarating, draining yet refreshing experiences.

What are we so desperately looking for that we will sit still Sunday after Sunday really listening to some preacher?

We are looking for life.

We are looking for the "truth."

We are looking for ourselves.

But, the rest of that story is that we are looking for God.

Augustine, long ago, was right: we are never going to be at peace until we find the way to God. Of course, we don't all realize that. And none of us knows it all the time. So we look for other things—for love, for money, for success, for "happiness," for fame, often just for whatever strikes our fancy at the moment. Sometimes we find what we are looking for—fame, fortune, or whatever—but it is never enough.

The rest of *that* story, of course, is that the only *enough* is God. We are never going to be satisfied with anything else. "You have made us for yourself [O God]," Augustine said, "and our hearts will remain restless until we are at rest in you" (*Confessions* 1.1; my translation).

So we keep on looking, looking for God. Even on a Sunday at church, listening to a sermon. That's why I keep on looking for the rest of the story in the hope of better telling the old, old story.

I find at least some of the rest of the story in unusual places. God sometimes comes to us—perhaps always—in unusual ways, unexpected ways. God doesn't always behave the way we think God should behave.

Several years ago, Dean of the Chapel Rick Wilson at Mercer University asked me to preach for a chapel service. It was to be in early December, just before Christmas. In my search for some way to tell the story in chapel just before Christmas, my eye fell on a gaudy little piece of bric-a-brac that sits atop a bookshelf in my office. It is a handmade something-or-other constructed of two scraps of wood and some assorted small pine cones all glued together. It is not even painted. But laboriously scratched in pencil on one side of the blocks of wood are the words

HAPPY FATHER'S DAY 1977
FROM ... BETH , BECCA , EDDIE

That's *the rest of the story* about that homemade, nondescript object—I don't even know what to call it—that sits prominently on top of a shelf in my office where I see it every day. Where it came from, what it means, gives that object a value beyond pricing.

Seeing that gift, it occurred to me that gifts and giving are what Christmas is all about. It is the rest of the story. So in chapel that day I told about the "Christmas Package" in which we may find some of the rest of the story about Christmas.

I am grateful that many other preachers are looking for the rest of the story also. Sometimes they help me find fresh ways to tell the story.

One Mother's Day a few years ago, during an interim pastorate, I went again to those familiar words of King Lemuel in Proverbs 31. Years earlier (1964), I had discovered M.K.W. Heicher's retelling of that story as "The Beauty That Is Not Vain" in the *Minister's Manual* and used his outline and even an illustration. But in the process of rereading and restudying Proverbs 31, I saw something I had never really seen before, something that seemed to me to be some of the rest of the story.

The words of Proverbs 31 are not a man's words, not King Lemuel's words—not according to the inscription. The inscription says these ancient words were those "with which his mother admonished him" (New Jewish Translation). That this ancient warning against the wrong kind of woman and then the ancient poem in praise of the right kind of woman were *from mother to son* makes a difference in the way those words should be understood, then and now. It is the rest of the story that makes plain the whole. Of course, I made Heicher's outline my own, and I gave a new title to my version ("Clear to the Bone"), but it was the rest of the story that really helped me tell it again.

We do find God in unusual places. And we often find the rest of the story in unusual places.

That is not unusual. We can, of course, find God in all the usual places, the places familiar to us: in the Bible, at church, at home, even in the wide world all around.

But we can miss God in all the usual places, also, simply because we already have an idea of what we are looking for, or an idea of what we ought to be looking for. When we find *that* god, the god we have defined or have had defined for us, we usually end up with the wrong god.

Finally, let me say a few words about husbands and wives and home and family and children. As of June 1997, all three of our own children are now married. All three of our children asked me to help with their wedding services, and in particular to prepare and deliver a wedding homily. All three of those homilies are included here.

The preaching task has always been awesome and not a little terrifying to me. But, frankly, I have never felt so inadequate as when I had to stand before our children and say something to them about—really—the rest of their lives. I tried as best I could to do for them what I have been trying for years to do: to discover some of the "rest of the story" regarding marriage and home and family. I hope those three pieces of the rest of the story were helpful to them in understanding and appreciating the whole story. I hope those words will be helpful for others also.

Sometimes finding the rest of the story helps get me back in the right way, back on track.

These lessons, homilies, and meditations—whatever you may name these little pieces of the story—have helped me. They seem also to have helped some others. I hope they will help you.

Edd Rowell
August 1997

Christmas Package

Isaiah 9:1-7; John 1:9-18; Luke 2:34-35

The Word became a Human Being—he pitched his tent, taber-
nacled, among us—full of Grace and Truth. And we saw his
Glory, the only-of-its-kind Glory, as from the Father.
                                        —John 1:14 (my paraphrase)

In 1977, I received a package with a gift inside. The giftwrap con-
sisted of the middle section of the Sunday funnies. It was rather
bumpily wrapped. It was beribboned with two scraps of string
tied together to make one piece long enough to go 'round the
knobbly gift inside and the ungainly wrap on the outside. I wish
I'd saved the package. I did save the string, and the gift inside.

To the right of my desk, prominently displayed atop a bookshelf, is a pitiful-looking object. I see it every day. It's two scraps
of wood glued together, with an assortment of pine cones glued
on top.

To me it's beautiful. And—assuming it has to be psychophysi-
cal to be artistic—it "speaks" to me. That gaudy little bric-a-brac
in its gaudier package was a gift—lovingly designed and carefully
constructed of the very best materials available—a gift from two
little girls and a little boy, ages eight, six, and three, to their
father.[1] Until it turns to dust, or I do, I will treasure it. Just for
what it is, even more for what it "says" to me.

I tell you a parable.

Christmas is about gifts, gifts that come in packages. Sometimes unlikely gifts in unseemly packages. Whether the package
and the gift are seemly or not, likely or not, is always—not just
sometimes—*always* a matter of perspective.

Jesus was unlikely to most, even unseemly to many. If *you*
were looking for some Word from God, would you look in a
cowstall, or on a cross?

Today, perhaps you would. *Now* you know where to look. But suppose you didn't have your New Testament roadmap? Suppose the only available directions pointed you toward a "Wonderful Counselor, Mighty God, Everlasting Father, Prince of Peace" with the government slung over his shoulder (Isa 9:6)? Would you be looking for a baby drooling in a cowstall, or for a grown-up bleeding on a cross?

Suppose you hadn't read this, and one day you walked into my office and saw that gaudy little piece of bric-a-brac beside my desk. Would you realize that ungainly collection of assorted scraps is an *objet d'art* of great value? Even so, many persons have yet to really *see* the Word that has come to us from God, in a cowstall, on a cross.

This "package" containing God's gift to us was indeed most unlikely and exceedingly unseemly. But God is apt to do things in rather unlikely ways that don't always fit our lofty conceptions of what is right and seemly.

The Word became a human being, John says. He pitched his tent among us. Prior to that, we had only *heard* about God, about humankind, about life, and all that. Hearsay, secondhand information. Now—as with Job of old—having before only *heard* by the hearing of our ears, *now* we can *see* with our eyes (Job 42:5). And everyone knows that just one object of art is worth many, many words.

It is a matter of perspective. The package was not just a baby in a manger, but a grown-up on a cross. (The symbol of our faith is after all not a cushioned manger in a warm cowstall but a cold cross on a rugged hill.) The Word became a human being—calluses, hangnails, split ends, flaky dandruff, and all—and lived among us. God does sometimes package things in unlikely, even unseemly ways. But perhaps most unlikely is what's inside. The Gift. The Word.

Exegetes have exegeted, and expositors have expounded whole libraries on the subject of that Word. Art, like beauty, is in the eye of the beholder, they say.[2] It means what it may mean. Well, what does *this* mean? What is the significance for us? Let me suggest three things.

The package and the gift inside say
Something about God.

Not everything about God. The only gods we can know every-thing about are the gods we make ourselves.

Harry Emerson Fosdick once suggested[3] the package shows us the "nearer end" of God, the part of God that has touched us. Picture a person on an island who can see and know the little piece of the great ocean that touches that little island. That small part is *not all* the whole great ocean; but it *is* the ocean, the "near end" of the ocean. Just so, Jesus is for us the "near end" of God.

Whatever else Jesus may say to us about God, there is grace, acceptance, forgiveness, love. In a word, Jesus shows us that God is *for* us. He shows us that no matter how far we may be, God runs to welcome us when we come to ourselves and turn toward home. Whatever else, we can at least know *that* about God. We can see it in Jesus, the "near end" of God for us.

But the package and the gift inside also tell us
Something about ourselves.

It says we are *worth Jesus*. We are *worth saving*. That's one certain word for us in this Jesus package.

This word may be harder to believe and accept than even what Jesus tells us about God. If I believe God at all, eventually I can learn to accept almost any godly thing about him. But in Jesus, God tells us that you and I are very valuable, we are *worth Jesus*.

You may have a healthy sense of self-worth by the standards of psychotherapeutic theory. But by any standard, that we are worth Jesus is difficult to really hear. Yet that's exactly what God's Word in Jesus tells us about ourselves. And not just about you and me, but about *every* person.

Finally, the package and the gift say
Something about right-living and wrong-living,
about running away and coming home,
about sin and salvation.

We have overheard the word that we somehow are made "in the image of God." Whatever else that may mean, it means we are made somehow *like God*. But what does *that* mean?

Just look inside the Christmas package. It means we are made to be *like Jesus*.

We can never comprehend all that God is. But God has uncovered Himself in Jesus. We *can* see the "near end" of God. A baby in a cowstall. A grown-up on a cross. And, at times, a person whom laughing children run to, grieving mothers and fathers turn to, and addicted madmen, ashamed outcasts, proud Pharisees, shameless Sadducees, persons fallen and cowardly, good people and bad people—everyone in fact who really sees Jesus—they all come to him, and he turns none away. Because he was not against but *for* all of them.

That's a lot of image to be made like!

Yet that's the very word we hear and the Word we see in Jesus. To be *really* you, to be *really* human, is to be *like Jesus*.

That's also the word about sin. Sin is the distortion, the perversion of that image. Sin, the New Testament says, is "missing the mark." What mark? What's the goal we're after? Just to be ourselves, to be really human. To whiningly complain that we are "only human" is not an excuse for but a judgment of wrong-living.

The best definition of sin is in Jesus' story about the loving father and the two prodigal sons. Unlike the older prodigal, the younger, runaway prodigal "came to himself" (Luke 15:17), and then went home. That he came to himself suggests he somehow was beside or outside or away from himself: that is, when he ran away from home he ran away from himself.

That's *exactly* what sin is. It is to be *beside* or *outside* or *away from* one's real, God-intended self.

The runaway son had a loving, longing, forgiving father to show him the way back to himself. So do we. And our Father-God has even given us a life-sized portrait, full-scale assembly instructions, to show us who we are and thus to help us find our way back to ourselves. Jesus. The Word. The Near End of God. The Package and the Gift.

When old Simeon held the baby Jesus in his arms, he said that baby would one day make known the Truth that would require decision and render judgment (Luke 2:34-35). Jesus did just that. He still does.

In our Christmas package, the Word makes known to us the truth about God, the truth about ourselves, and the truth that the one is waiting with open arms for the other to come home.

Christmas gift! Amen.

Failure Need Not Be Fatal

A Maundy Thursday Lesson

Matthew 27:1-5; Luke 23:39-43; John 8:3-11; 1 John 1:5—2:2

When morning came, all the chief priests and the elders of the people conferred together against Jesus in order to bring about his death. They bound him, led him away, and handed him over to Pilate the governor.

When Judas, his betrayer, saw that Jesus was condemned, he repented and brought back the thirty pieces of silver to the chief priests and the elders. He said, "I have sinned by betraying innocent blood." But they said, "What is that to us? See to it yourself." Throwing down the pieces of silver in the temple, he departed; and he went and hanged himself.

—Matthew 27:1-5 RSV

That's how Matthew sums up the failure of Judas. But John the Elder best tells why Judas's failure, as well as the failure of any of us, need not be fatal.

This is the message we have heard from him and proclaim to you, that God is light and in him is no darkness at all. If we say that we have fellowship with him while we are walking in darkness, we lie and do not do what is true; but if we walk in the light as he himself is in the light, we have fellowship with one another, and the blood of Jesus his Son cleanses us from all sin. If we say that we have no sin, we deceive ourselves, and the truth is not in us. If we confess our sins, he who is faithful and just will forgive us our sins and cleanse us from all unrighteousness. If we say that we have not sinned, we make him a liar, and his word is not in us.

My little children, I am writing these things to you so that you may not sin. But if anyone does sin, we have an advocate with the Father, Jesus Christ the righteous; and he is the atoning sacrifice for our sins, and not for ours only but also for the sins of the whole world.

—1 John 1:5–2:2 RSV

Let us back up and repeat that one line that among all the rest most bears repeating and remembering.

> If we confess our sins, he is just and may be trusted to forgive our sins and cleanse us from every kind of wrongdoing.
>   —1 John 1:9 REB

I don't know how long I've been thinking about Judas Iscariot, along with, of course, Simon Peter. Peter denied Jesus. Judas betrayed Jesus. Both of them failed. They failed Jesus. They failed themselves. They failed us. And everyone of us can—sooner or later—identify with that.

The usual thing is to identify with Peter. Blustering, bumbling, foot-in-mouth Peter. One time when his life was on the line, Peter failed fearfully (or fearfully failed). Our 20/20 hindsight can understand Peter's failure. We can even forgive him for it—his life, after all, was really at risk. We can identify with him because of that, especially since later on when Peter's life was again in danger he played the hero.

But finally, we can identify with Peter, not just because we can understand and even excuse Peter for his failure, but because Peter's failure was not fatal.

I don't know how long I've been thinking about these things, about Judas and Peter and Jesus, trying to sort out why Judas's failure was fatal and Peter's was not. I've learned along the way that a lot of other people have been thinking about Judas and Peter also. And I have run into all kinds of explanations regarding why Peter failed though not fatally, and why Judas fatally failed.

The reason Peter failed, the reason he denied Jesus—not just once but three times, and with curses—is rather simple. Peter was afraid for his life. He did the wrong thing. He took the coward's way out. You and I would never do something like that. . . . Or would we?

It is alright to say such things out loud, just as it is also alright to whistle a happy tune when on a dark and stormy night you have to walk home alone . . . through the woods . . . by the cemetery. It's alright. It is even alright to pretend we believe each other when we make such childish claims. It's alright.

But in the solitary sincerity and solemn sanctuary of our own hearts, you and I know better. If we had been in Peter's place, we like Peter probably would have done everything we could to save ourselves. Peter, along with all the disciples, was in danger of losing his life. He saved himself. Later on, Peter was steadfast in his loyalty to Jesus, even in a just-as-dangerous, life-threatening situation. But that first time, Peter saved himself, even when the price he had to pay for his life was the repeated denial of Jesus.

Still we can identify with Peter. Peter saved himself. Peter survived, as we say, to fight, to risk his life, another day. We can understand why Peter failed. We don't like it. And we would like to pretend that it could never happen to us. But we can understand.

I don't know for how long I've been thinking about Peter and Judas, trying to figure out why they could have failed, and what is the lesson for me. I know I have encountered all kinds of explanations for the failure of Judas, why he betrayed Jesus.

Some of the great Bible students of the early church—Chrysostom, Origen, Thomas Aquinas—and even some Bible scholars of our own time are convinced it was purely for greed, thirty pieces of silver. The writer of 1 Timothy (6:10) said that "the love of money is a root of all kinds of evil." Even long before that, Amos spoke of selling "the righteous for silver, and the needy for a pair of sandals" (2:6), and Ezekiel (13:19) told of profaning God "for handfuls of barley and for pieces of bread." Greed indeed is the root of all kinds of evil.

> Still as of old
> Man by himself is priced,
> For thirty pieces Judas sold
> Himself, not Christ.[4]

But is that really why Judas sold his soul? For thirty pieces of silver? It was a substantial sum—about the going price for an average slave. But it was not *that* substantial. It was not enough to make Judas rich. And, think about it, Judas had already given up

his own life, along with whatever he had at home, to become a
follower of Jesus. Besides, someone who is motivated only by
greed would not throw away money as Judas did.

Greed simply doesn't explain Judas.

Some Bible students have even suggested Judas was ambi-
tious for leadership and jealous of the prominence of Peter,
James, and John. Some say he was vindictive, trying to get back
at Jesus for singling him out for criticism. Remember, Jesus had
rebuked Judas for complaining that the ointment Mary rubbed on
Jesus' feet was wasted. Was Judas that jealous, that vindictive?

I don't know how long I've been thinking about this, trying to
figure out why Judas did what he did to Jesus and to himself. The
Devil made him do it? Yes, just as the Devil made Peter do what
he did and made the Scribes and Pharisees do what they did, just
as the Devil makes you and me do some of the things we do.

Back in 1929, a Jewish rabbi named Jacob Golub wrote a
book for high school students entitled *In the Days of the Second
Temple*. In that little book the rabbi suggested that Judas was not
a traitor but a patriot. Judas, the rabbi said, was the only one
among Jesus' disciples who recognized what a dangerous revolutionary Jesus really was. Judas was a good Jew, so he turned Jesus
in to the authorities.

It was as if one of us realized that some religious leader was
really promoting a movement that would overthrow the government. As a loyal citizen we might very well give information to
the FBI. Judas didn't necessarily think Jesus would be executed,
only that he would be silenced and his revolutionary movement
stopped. Judas and Paul, Rabbi Golub would say, had a lot in common. They were both good Jews, and they fought to save Judaism
from the revolutionary teachings of Jesus.[5]

I think it is quite possible that Judas acted impulsively, impa-
tiently. Judas was a believer. He believed Jesus when Jesus said it
was time for the kingdom to come on earth as in heaven. But just
like all the rest of the disciples (see Acts 1:6), Judas misunder-
stood. Judas expected an earthly kingdom. He wanted Jesus to
take over, to kick the Romans out of Palestine, and to install himself in Jerusalem as king of the Jews—just like *the good old days*.

Judas got impatient and maybe a little frustrated with Jesus. So he tried to force Jesus' hand. He tried to make Jesus use his God-given powers. He turned Jesus in to the authorities so Jesus would be forced to defend himself and take over. It didn't work. Judas could not force Jesus to use force. And when he saw his scheme had gone sour, he tried desperately to give the money back and save Jesus. When he failed in that, his depression, his guilt, was complete, and he committed suicide.

I don't know how long I've been thinking about Judas and Peter and Jesus, trying to figure it all out. I know I have been thinking about it at least since 1978 when I enlisted Beth, Becca, and Eddie to help me write a book about the apostles for middle children.[6] I'd never written anything for children before that. But with the help of our children, I managed to get through Peter, James, John, and all the rest.

Then we got to Judas. How do you explain Judas to a child? What kind of lesson can Judas teach a child? We finally wrote down that "Judas was sorry too late," that what Judas did was terribly wrong, that Judas was sorry, but he was too late with his sorry. But that explanation of Judas and that lesson is at best only provisional. At worst, it may be dishonest. You see, all these years I've been focusing on the wrong thing. I've been focusing on Judas's failure, Judas's sin. But that cannot explain why Judas's failure was fatal. It is the wrong lesson.

I don't know how long I've been thinking about Judas and Peter and Jesus, trying to figure it all out.

Ray Anderson is pastor of Harbour Fellowship in Huntington Beach, California, and also professor of theology and ministry at Fuller Theological Seminary in Pasadena. Ray Anderson says he has been thinking about Judas Iscariot for more than twenty years. Then one day, Ray Anderson says, he was in San Francisco, in a restroom, when he looked up to see some startling words printed in block letters with a blue felt-tip marker across the top of the mirror:

JUDAS COME HOME—ALL IS FORGIVEN![7]

Ray Anderson says he still hasn't figured it out. Who would write such a thing? And why? What does it mean? Oh, he has tried all kinds of theories to explain how those words got there and why. But finally he realized that at least one reason for those startling, shocking, outrageous words was to make him think about it.

Could it really be true? Can God forgive anything and everything? *Does* God forgive anything and everything? Is this gospel or heresy? Judas come home—all is forgiven?

Well, Anderson finally wrote a book about it. It is the only book I have ever purchased sight unseen and solely because of the title. I had no idea until the book arrived from out West whether the contents would live up to the title. The title is *The Gospel according to Judas*. You've heard of the Gospel according to Matthew, Mark, Luke, John. This is the Gospel according to Judas. And the lesson for us is that Judas's sin—or Peter's sin or your sin or my sin—is not the point at all. It is not what is important. And trying to understand the whys and wherefores of our sins is to miss the real truth altogether. The real point—as John the Elder so clearly put it—is that "if we confess our sins to God, he will keep his promise and do what is right: he will forgive us our sins and purify us from all our wrongdoing" (1 John 1:9 TEV).

That's the point. *That's* the lesson. It explains why Peter's failure was *not* fatal. It explains why Judas's failure *was* fatal. One lesson for us is that failure—any failure—on our part need not ever be fatal.

Anderson ends his book with an imagined monologue by Judas. Finally, Judas says to us,

> I was wrong when I assumed that my betrayal had caused [Jesus'] death. I was wrong to inflict upon myself the terrible burden of bearing my own sin and so destroy myself through guilt. And you would be wrong to feel that the cross of Jesus Christ stands over against you as a sign of his innocence and your guilt. Neither your sins nor mine *caused* him to die on the cross. In allowing himself to be put to death without resistance, he did bear the consequence of our sins. But he did this *because of God's love for us and because of his love and obedience to God,*

his Father. We're mistaken when we think that it was our sin, not the love of God, that brought Jesus to the point of his own death. . . .

Why did I not remember the words of Jesus when I needed most to hear and believe them? I have tried to tell you, and to warn you as well as encourage you. My assumptions were all wrong, my thinking twisted, my reasons irrational.

But he found me, and with his finger dipped in the darkness of my own despair, wrote on the glass where I expected to see only my own lonely face:

JUDAS COME HOME—ALL IS FORGIVEN![8]

Amen.

Exalted Humility

A Palm Sunday Lesson

Zechariah 9:9-10; Mark 11:1-11; Philippians 2:5-11

Let the same mind be in you that was in Christ Jesus.
—Philippians 2:5 NRSV

I have been working at Mercer University Press since August 1980. Until October 1994, our offices were on the main campus, a convenient ten-minute drive from home. But since we moved out on Peake Road on the northwest perimeter of Macon, I have quite a drive to and from work each day. In the morning I don't notice it so much: not many folks are on the road as early as I go to work. But at lunchtime and in the evenings it gets a little hairy driving down Zebulon Road and then down Forsyth Road, Ridge Avenue, and finally Ingleside Avenue to get home. You really have to watch out for folks who seem determined to run you over.

It is especially apparent on the two-lane sections of the drive. Unless you are driving at least ten or fifteen mph *over* the speed limit, someone will get right on your rear bumper and do their best to push you out of the way or at least to harass you into going faster. Then on the four-lane sections of Forsyth, everyone seems determined to get in front of the line before the four-lane narrows again to a two-lane.

It is rude to break in line at the grocery checkout or someplace else; of course, in some cases it also may be risky. But it is downright dangerous to try to break in line on Zebulon Road or Forsyth Road at lunchtime or in the evening just after dark. Some of those folks never heard of the last being first and the first being last.

I don't know about you, but I need Palm Sunday. Palm Sunday came just in time for me this year. I've been driving up and down Forsyth Road and Zebulon Road and almost getting run over in the process, and I need Palm Sunday.

Palm Sunday reminds me that humility and just a little consideration for others is really the best policy. Because Palm Sunday reminds me of Jesus who came riding into town on a donkey. Not on six white horses, not even in a Chevrolet. And certainly not ten to fifteen mph over the speed limit. But on a donkey, a humble mode of transportation then or anytime.

I know they laid palm branches and even their garments before him and clapped and shouted and sang and cheered as he rode into town. But he was riding on a donkey! The lowliest of the low. The humblest of the humble.

I commend to you Palm Sunday, and the picture of Jesus the Lord Christ riding into town on the back of a donkey. Picture a scrawny little donkey with Jesus astraddle and with Jesus' legs almost dragging the ground.

Got the picture. Good. We need to be reminded.

The Palm Sunday lesson in Mark's Gospel (11:1-11) and the passage in the Old Testament (Zech 9:9-10), which is the prophetic background for Palm Sunday, tell the story. But one lesson that really explains Palm Sunday is Philippians 2:5-11.

The churchfolk at Philippi needed a Palm Sunday, too. Nobody knows exactly what was going on at Philippi. Maybe they were breaking in line or trying to run each other off the road on their way to and from work.

Something was going on at Philippi. From the tone of his letter to the folks at Philippi, we know that Philippi was one of Paul's favorites and the folks there were his good friends and helpers. Paul had a special place in his heart for Philippi: "I thank my God every time I remember you," he told them (1:3). Still in the best of families and in the best of churches, problems sometimes arise. Nobody knows exactly what those problems were at First Church Philippi. But we do know there were some disagreements and hurt feelings and even broken relationships in the church.

Paul singles out two of the Philippians—the two women named Euodia [yoo-oh-dee-uh] and Syntyche [sin-tye-kee] (4:2).

Names in the Bible mean something, and the meaning of a name is usually significant. For example, the name "Jesus" means "he will save" or "savior"; that's why the angel told Joseph to call him "Jesus/Savior, for he will save his people from their sins" (Matt 1:21).

Well, Euodia means "good journey" or "fine traveler," and Syntyche means "coincidence" or "accident." It certainly sounds like the "good driver" Euodia and the "accident-prone" Syntyche could have been having trouble on the road. Maybe Syntyche was tailgating Euodia, and Euodia was determined not to let Syntyche pass. At any rate, those two women in particular had troubles at Philippi.

Paul doesn't tell just Syntyche and Euodia; he tells the whole church they need to get their heads together and get their minds on the same wavelength. "Let the same mind be in you," Paul said, "that was in Christ Jesus" (2:5). Then of course, in 2:6-11, he goes on to tell them what kind of mind was in Christ Jesus.

Paul said that, even though he deserved it, Jesus did not grab for the honor and glory that rightly belonged to him. He didn't break in line. He didn't push anybody off the road. He didn't even tailgate anybody. Instead, Paul said, Jesus became a servant, in human form, and became obedient to God up to and including the worst kind of dying anyone could imagine—death on a cross.

Jesus told his disciples that "the greatest among you will be your servant" (Matt 23:11). And later, after Jesus had washed his disciples' feet, he said that "I have set you an example, that you also should do as I have done to you" (John 13:15). "So if I, your Lord and Teacher, have washed your feet," Jesus said, "you also ought to wash one another's feet" (John 13:14).

There has been a lot of discussion over the years about what Paul meant when he told the Philippians to get their heads straight and to "let the same mind be in you that was in Christ Jesus." Maybe I don't comprehend the complexities of it, but it seems rather plain to me. What Paul meant was that the Philippians were to remember who they were and to get on about the business of following the example of the one they claimed as Lord, that same Jesus who chose to be a servant unto death.

I say all that to say that Palm Sunday came just in time for me this year. I suspect it may have come just in time for you also. We need Palm Sunday to remind us of Jesus riding into Jerusalem on a donkey—his legs wrapped round that lowly beast, and his feet almost dragging the ground. Easter is coming, for sure. The first disciples did not know to expect Easter. In fact, at first they didn't even believe Easter when it did come. But we know Easter is coming. We know what to expect. We even look forward to it.

But we must not let the anticipation of Easter blind us to the fact that Palm Sunday—Jesus on a lowly donkey—and Good Friday—Jesus hanging on a cross—are two of the places that Jesus *and we* have to travel through in order to get to Easter.

I was born and raised in LA—Lower Alabama. The place I was born and raised and call "down home" is so far back in the woods I tell folks it is not on the way to anywhere. You can't get there by accident. You have to be deliberately going there to get there. And you have to get there by way of Luverne and Brantley and Dozier and Gantt and then Andalusia and finally by way of Bogan's Level.

Well, Easter is a lot like that. We can't get to Easter from just anywhere. Not even by accident. We have to go by way of Palm Sunday and Maundy Thursday and Good Friday and Dark Saturday to get to Easter Sunday.

In his "Palm Sunday lesson" to the Philippians, Paul went on to tell them that, eventually, God "highly exalted" the humble servant Jesus, and that "at the name of Jesus every knee should bend, in heaven and on earth and under the earth, and every tongue should confess that Jesus Christ is Lord, to the glory of God the Father" (Phil 2:10-11). Easter, eventually, does follow Palm Sunday and Maundy Thursday and Good Friday and Dark Saturday.

Jesus insisted on riding into Jerusalem on a donkey, and he insisted on washing his disciples' feet. He did it, at least in part, to show us the way to Easter, to show us how the Easter-life is lived, to give us an example to follow.

I need Palm Sunday. You need Palm Sunday. We all need Palm Sunday. To remind us who we are, and who we ought to be. And to remind us that we need to get our heads straight and our minds right and get on with the business of serving God and blessing our Lord Christ and helping, not running over, each other.

Jesus came riding into town one day on the back of a donkey. Not on six white horses. Not in a grand chariot. Not even in a Ford. He came on a donkey.

Then he washed his disciples' feet.

And he died on a cross.

We need Palm Sunday, Maundy Thursday, Good Friday, and Black Saturday. Because that's the way to Easter. It's the only way.

I'm glad Palm Sunday has come round again, just in time. I need all the reminding I can get.

I suspect you do too.

Now I'm on the way to Easter.

Come, go with me. Amen.

Thomas's Question, Easter's Answer

An Easter Lesson

John 20:19-31

But Thomas . . . was not with them when Jesus came.
—John 20:24 NRSV

Thomas answered him, "My Lord and my God!"
—John 20:28 NRSV

Doubt is part of religion. All the religious thinkers were doubters.[9]
—Isaac Bashevis Singer

Once in a while we hear a sermon or a Sunday school lesson that focuses on Peter. Invariably, the preacher or teacher will suggest that all of us can identify with Peter. Peter—brash, emotional, self-assertive Peter. Peter, who—because he feared for his life—denied he even knew Jesus, not once but three times, and loudly. But who later overcame his fears and became just as loud and just as assertive in telling others about Jesus.

We can all identify with Peter. At least we can identify with Peter-the-fearful who denied Jesus. We know we ought to be able to identify with Peter-the-fearless who told everyone about Jesus. Peter is a good example. All of us who claim Christ as Lord know we have failed our Lord, probably more than just three times. And not in fear for our lives, but most likely just in fear of being ridiculed or ostracized in a world that still neither understands nor appreciates Jesus. And all of us timidly expect or desperately hope that the next time we will have the courage to do the right thing, to stand up for Jesus, to be true to our Lord and to ourselves—just like Peter.

Peter is a good example for all of us. That's why we preachers and teachers keep on holding him up, and why we keep on reminding that all of us can identify with Peter.

Even on Easter we might hold up Peter as an example. After the Resurrection, Peter went fishing (21:3). But just as soon as Jesus called to the disciples from the seashore, Peter didn't wait for anybody else, not even for the boat: he jumped in and swam to shore to get to Jesus first.

We can identify with that. After Easter it will be back to business as usual for us, too, back to our fishing boats and nets. But if Jesus shows up, we will probably jump to get to him first and find out what he wants us to do. At least we would like to think we will put down our fishing poles and jump at the chance to find out what Jesus wants us to do.

Even on Easter—which is the answer to some of the most important questions in life—Peter is a good example.

Any *church* in the world in any age can find its portrait hanging in the gallery of the "seven churches" in Revelation 1–3, because those seven turned out to be not just seven churches in first-century Asia, but prototypes of all the churches of every age and every location.

We can say the same thing about the *people* who surrounded Jesus: if you look carefully enough, you will find your own portrait in the gallery of the saints and sinners around Jesus. It may be a composite portrait. You may see yourself in more than one of the saints and sinners who populate the gospel stories. But your portrait *is there somewhere*. Maybe you really are like Peter. Or Martha. Or the Woman of Samaria. Or even "Lebbaeus called Thaddaeus" but whose real name was Judas and about whom we know little else except that he had at least three names.

Maybe you are or would like to be like one of the Marys who went early to the cemetery, discovered the empty tomb, and ran to tell the disciples. Perhaps you see yourself in anxious Peter who ran to the garden tomb to see for himself. Or you may identify with Mr. or Mrs. Cleopas, who had an unforgettable experience at their supper table in Emmaus, an experience they had to get up and go tell everyone about.

With which portrait in the gospel stories do you identify?

Let me mention one more person. Thomas or Didymus, the one referred to as "the twin." (We *don't know* who he was twin to.

Some Bible students have suggested he was brother to one of the other disciples; some say he had a twin sister; some have even said he was Jesus' twin.)

Before you take offense, let me tell you I think Thomas has had more criticism than he really deserves. I know it is not very flattering to be called a "doubting Thomas," but I am not so sure Thomas deserves our scorn.

We don't know a lot about Thomas. We don't know much about a lot of folks in the gospel stories. But we know enough. Thomas appears in every list of Jesus' disciples, and he is listed with Peter and the rest who went fishing after the resurrection. Otherwise, Thomas figures in only three incidents, all of them recorded only by John.

Remember how Jesus was summoned when Lazarus was sick but didn't go until after Lazarus died? Evidently most of the disciples did not want to go back to Judah for fear of the Jews (11:8). But Jesus insisted on going. And Thomas led the way for the other disciples when he said, "Let us also go, even if we have to die with him" (11:16, my translation). There's nothing doubtful about *that* Thomas. He led the way for the others to follow and to do the right thing.

A little later Jesus and his disciples had their last supper together and their last intimate conversation. Jesus told them he was going on ahead to make a place for them. He told them they already knew the way to the place he was preparing for them. But Thomas spoke up and said, "Lord, we don't know where you're going. How can we know the way?" (14:5).

For that question, Thomas has been accused of being everything from dumb to insensitive to unbelieving. But have you noticed that Thomas's question set the stage for one of the most important statements Jesus ever made? "I am the way, and the truth, and the life. No one comes to the Father except through me" (14:6).

I can remember when I was in school, way back in the olden times, how I was often grateful when someone else asked the very question I was anxious to ask but was afraid to ask for fear of appearing dumb.

Thanks to Thomas for asking the question. That's how we get answers.

And consider that Thomas may have deliberately asked the question just so the rest of the "class" could hear the answer.

Finally, John tells us about the appearance of Jesus to all the disciples. It was on the same day Mary and the others discovered the empty tomb, that is, on the first Easter, in the evening. They were all shut up in the house, perhaps the house where John Mark lived, and probably in the guest room upstairs, that famous "upper room" (Mark 14:15; Luke 22:12). Jesus had been crucified on Friday. On that Sunday Jesus' followers were afraid they might be next. So the doors were shut tight and locked, "for fear of the Jews," John said (20:19). John went on to say that "Jesus came and stood among them and said, 'Peace be with you.' After he said this, he showed them his hands and his side. Then the disciples rejoiced when they saw the Lord" (20:19-20). That's one of our favorite Easter stories. Do you remember what follows?

"Thomas," John said, "was not with them when Jesus came" (20:24). So the other disciples told Thomas about Jesus' appearing to them: "We have seen the Lord," they said (20:25a). That's when Thomas made the remark he is most famous for: "Unless I see the mark of the nails in his hands, and put my finger in the mark of the nails and my hand in his side, I will not believe" (20:25b).

That's what we remember about Thomas. That's where that unflattering phrase "doubting Thomas" comes from. But it's time we rescued Thomas from that deep, dark hole he's been thrown into. We need to remember what Paul Harvey calls "the rest of the story," the rest of the story that really explains the whole story.

The rest of the story of course is what happened later. John wrote that "a week later [Jesus'] disciples were again in the [same] house, and Thomas was with them" (20:26), when Jesus appeared to them again. Evidently having heard what Thomas had said, Jesus invited Thomas to touch him and see that he was real.

Thomas didn't have to touch. He just fell to his knees and confessed, "My Lord and my God!" (20:28). Jesus responded that those who "come to believe," even though they don't see Jesus in the flesh, will be blessed. That's when John added his explanation that all the gospel stories were told "so that you may come to believe that Jesus is the Messiah, the Son of God, and that through believing you may have life in his name" (20:31).

You see, the confession of Thomas—"My Lord and my God!"—is really the climax of the Gospel of John. That confession is the purpose of the whole gospel story—that those who hear the story might believe and through believing might have life.

Don't look with disfavor on Thomas. Thomas was a leader among the disciples when they were afraid. Thomas asked some of the right questions at the right time so you and I may benefit from answers to questions we need answers to. And Thomas said out loud what all of us probably have thought: "This is too good to be true." After all, it's when we have the good sense to think something is too good to be true that we learn for sure it is too good *not* to be true.

Easter really is the answer to our deepest questions. Long ago, in his melancholy, Job asked, "If a person dies, shall that person live again?" That's not just Job's question. It was Thomas's question. It is your question and mine. Easter says, Yes. "Because I live," Jesus said, "you also will live" (14:18).

That's Easter's answer to life's great question. All of us are aching to know that answer. Many of us are afraid to ask the question, afraid of the world's ridicule, or the world's scorn, or even the scorn of those who mistakenly think it is sinful to ask questions. But not Thomas. He was not afraid to ask the right questions. He was not afraid even to express his doubts out loud.

From that point on we don't for sure know much about Thomas. Several different traditions say he carried the gospel to India and established churches there. (We do know that there are some strong churches in India that go back to the very beginnings of the church, in fact, back to the time of Thomas.) But I think Thomas's faith was stronger and his commitment deeper because he was not afraid to ask the questions to which all of us want answers.

Easter? Easter came just in time again this year, didn't it? Just in time to remind us that the important questions of life already have been answered, some of them in an upper room among folks just like you and me, frightened and shut up against the imagined and real hurts of the world. Some of those answers have come to us free of charge, with no risk of embarrassment or ridicule, because "questioning Thomas" had the good sense and the courage to ask out loud.

Yes, Thomas, Jesus is alive. And because Jesus lives, you will live also.

Just one more word.

The resurrection becomes real for you and for me only when Jesus lives and rules in our hearts and lives.

According to John, at least one reason Thomas asked questions was so you and I finally might believe, and declare with Thomas, "My Lord! My God!"

Is it resurrection for you yet? Amen.

Easter's Over, I'm Going Fishing

An After-Easter Lesson

John 21:1-19

Simon Peter said to them, "I am going fishing."
—John 21:3 NRSV

After this [Jesus] said to him, "Follow me."
—John 21:19 NRSV

John 21 is a puzzle. The Gospel of John already ends with chapter 20: "These things are written so you may come to believe that Jesus is Christ, the Son of God, and that by believing you may have life in him" (20:31). That's a good ending to the gospel story. It sums up the purpose and point of the gospel story in a single, clear, comprehensible statement. Then comes chapter 21. Why?

At the risk of seeming simplistic, let us just suppose John added chapter 21 because John had something more to say. It occurred to John there was something more to tell the disciples about discipleship. That something more is chapter 21. What more does John want us to know? . . . Let me tell you a story.

Easter is over. Jesus died, he appeared to the disciples and some others, and now he is gone again. Easter is over, Simon Peter says, "I'm going fishing." And the rest of the disciples went along with him.

To hear what some Bible students have said about this, you would think Peter and the other disciples committed the unpardonable sin.

An influential biblical theologian of an earlier generation (he died the year I was born) said, "The scene is one of complete apostasy, and is the fulfillment of [John] 16:32."[10] (In John 16:32 Jesus says the time is coming when the disciples will be scattered, everyone going his own way, forsaking Jesus.)

In his massive commentary on John, Raymond E. Brown said, "The scene is rather one of aimless activity undertaken in desperation."[11]

Never has a fishing trip come in for so much criticism. Peter and the rest, I think, have been falsely accused, and badly.

It was the most natural thing for the disciples to go fishing. After all, many of them were professional fishermen. That's what they did for a living. *That's who they were.*

For a long time now, these fishermen and others had been following Jesus around Galilee and Judea, right up to the moment he was arrested, tried and convicted, and executed. Even afterwards they were still together, a close-knit band of fishermen, tax collectors, and the like, who had decided to follow Jesus and to do so together.

Now Jesus was gone . . . again. Jesus was gone. What were they to do?

For one thing, life had to go on. Maybe they were uncertain about what they should do. Perhaps they were unsure of the future. After all, up to this time, ever since they had answered Jesus' call to come follow him, they had done just that—followed Jesus. Now Jesus was not there to tell them where to go or what to do.

"I'm going fishing," Peter said. It was the most natural thing in the world. And just as naturally, the others said, "Alright, we'll go with you."

There is nothing wrong with going back to work after Easter is over. In fact, that is what we should be doing. Life goes on. And part of life going on is our everyday work.

But there is a larger dimension to life. Jesus joined the disciples on their fishing trip, but then he got down to the business of reminding them that they were to follow him and be fishers for persons too.

Easter is over. I'm going fishing. For fish. And for people. The Resurrection has become real for me because Jesus lives in my heart. I want the Resurrection to be real for you too, and for everyone I can reach, whether at home, at work, at play, even at church, wherever my life may take me.

I'm going fishing. Come go with me. Amen.

Clear to the Bone

A Mother's Day Lesson

Proverbs 31:10-31

Charm is deceitful, and beauty is vain,
but a woman who fears the Lord is to be praised.
—Proverbs 31:30 NRSV

In many churches on Mother's Day King Lemuel will be speaking again. You remember "Lemuel, king of Massa."[12] He's the one whose ancient words we read in Proverbs 31:10-31.[13]

Who can find a virtuous/capable/good woman?
for her price is far above rubies. . . .
Her children rise up and call her blessed,
her husband also, and he praises her.

But these words are not really a man's words. They are not Lemuel's words. The inscription says these are the words "that *his mother taught him.*" And the lesson of these words is not just for mothers, but for all of us, mothers and fathers, sons and daughters.

We know very little about Lemuel. But to this day, his words reflect the glory of a good person, a wife and mother, whose beauty goes clear to the bone. A "good woman" may no longer make fine linen and sell it, but she does look well to the ways of her household. . . . So, for that matter, does a good man.

Note that these words appear in Proverbs, a book that doesn't always speak of wives and mothers with praise. In one place Proverbs says, "It is better to live in the desert than with a contentious, vexatious wife" (21:19 TNK). Or, "Like a gold ring in the snout of a pig is a beautiful woman bereft of sense" (11:22 TNK). Such critical words are in sharp contrast to the words of Lemuel. The words of Lemuel speak of a beauty that goes clear to the bone.

A young boy wanted something pretty for Mother's Day. He went to the lingerie department at Macy's. "I want to buy my mother a slip," he told the clerk. But when it came to the important information regarding size, the boy was at a loss. "It would help," the clerk told him, "if you could tell me whether your mother is tall or short, fat or slim." "Oh," he replied, "she's just perfect!" So the clerk wrapped a pretty slip—size 34—for the boy to take home to his mother. . . . On Monday his mother came in to exchange the slip for one that would fit.

Real beauty is independent of physical size or appearance. "Charm/Grace is deceptive," Proverbs says, "and beauty is vain /an illusion." Proverbs recognizes that physical, external beauty really is only skin deep. There is a beauty of personality that goes deeper and lasts longer than a pretty face. There is a grace of character that stands out more regally than mere physical posture.

It is that kind of beauty the boy saw in his "just-perfect" mother. It is infinitely more important than the other kind. The reason, of course, is that a pretty face or regal carriage cannot for long conceal an empty head or a hard heart; neither can a plain face nor even a bent frame hide the bright light of a beautiful spirit.

The old saying that "Beauty is only skin deep but ugly goes clear to the bone" is not the whole truth. Beauty goes clear to the bone also. In fact, unless it does, it is vain, empty. There is a beauty that is *not* vain, and we all would be healthier and happier and holier people if more of that beauty appeared in us all. Let's analyze it.

First, such beauty includes a certain wholeness.

Jesus once quoted part of the Jewish Shema (Deut 6:4-9)[14]: "You shall love the Lord your God with all your heart, and with all your soul, and with all your mind" (Matt 22:37; Mark 12:29; Luke 10:27). Most sermons I've heard on the text emphasize the parts—heart, soul, mind. But in fact the emphasis is on the "all," the *whole* person. Anyone who sets out to do anything halfway—especially life—is bound to come up short.

My father is a carpenter. He taught me how to cut a board. He said, "Son, always measure twice and saw once, and *always cut on the outside of the line*. You can cut a board shorter, but you can't cut it longer."

Life is like that. Many live life according to what is "legal," giving to life just enough to get by. They come up short, often in an ugly way. You can't live life partway, cutting it as close to the line as possible, and expect it to come out beautiful and worthwhile.

I'm convinced one reason for so much ugliness in our world today is that ours is a "part-time" generation. One reason for so much ugliness in some marriages is that we have so many part-time husbands and part-time wives. Homes come up short and get ugly because there are so many part-time fathers and part-time mothers and part-time children. Businesses, industries, governments, and almost everything else that requires some measure of wholehearted commitment are failing because so many upon whom their success depends are only part-time workers. Schools with part-time teachers and part-time students graduate only part-time adults, only partly educated to live out their lives only partway. And churches are only skin-deep churches if they have to depend on part-time Christians.

King Lemuel praised the wife and mother who "looked well to the ways of her household" (v. 27). But one real point of his praise was that this was a woman who gave herself wholly, completely, without reservation, to the living out of her life—and she was no "homebody." It was beautiful, not just skin deep but clear to the bone. Lemuel was talking about a woman he loved and cared for. But the lesson can apply to all of us. The beautiful life is marked by wholeness, wholeness of character, devotion, commitment—integrity, oneness.

Second, this beauty involves a certain harmony.

Wholeness without balance can be awkward, even ugly. There is a perfect picture of the crucial difference between awkwardness and balance in Luke's story of Mary and Martha (Luke 10:38-42). Martha—running every which way at once trying desperately to get the fried chicken and green beans and mashed potatoes and homemade rolls and Luzianne tea all done at the same time, while setting the table with one of her other hands, and touching up with a dustcloth with another. And there was her sister Mary, sitting on the rug in front of the company chair where Jesus was talking with all the other visitors while waiting on dinner.

"Jesus," Martha said, "don't you even care I'm having to do all the work while Mary is just sitting there bug-eyed. . . .? Why don't you tell her to get up and come help me." Martha—Luke said—was "distracted"[15] by all she had to do.

I've always been sympathetic for Martha. Martha was getting done what had to be done in order for life to go on: she was doing the work, paying the bills, bringing home the bacon, washing the dishes, making the beds, sweeping the floors—all those mundane things that make life liveable, even possible. *Somebody* has to get the work done and pay the bills, else we can't get on with the rest of life.

But Martha overdid it. What Martha was doing was good, necessary, helpful. She was doing her share, making a contribution. But she was running in so many directions getting all those good things done that she had lost sight of the best thing.

Jesus said Martha was "anxious and troubled about many things" when "few things are [really] needful, or only one [thing really is needful]" (Luke 10:41-42 RSV). What's important is to find life's central meaning and purpose, and let everything else revolve around that. Like an axle and a wheel, if the axle is off-center, then the movement of the wheel is troubled, and eventually it will self-destruct. Martha didn't have that center focus. She was torn apart because of that lack. So many people run around grabbing everything they can get their hands on, doing anything and everything that comes up, thinking that's the way to the full life. Yet for all their running to and fro, their lives are really going nowhere and accomplishing nothing because none of it has any meaning or purpose.

Lemuel's beautiful wife found a center in her "fear/worship of the Lord" (Prov 31:30); Mary found it sitting at Jesus' feet (Luke 10:39). In the final analysis, real harmony and balance in life can come only from obedience to the one whose purpose is to bring harmony into all creation, or, as Paul put it, to reconcile the world unto himself (2 Cor 5:19). Only with his help can we find the balance and harmony necessary for the kind of beauty in life that goes clear to the bone.

Finally, real beauty has a certain radiance about it.

The beautiful life glows with vitality; it sparkles with vibrance and light. The beautiful life, in other words, has hope at its center, a positive outlook on all life, because the beautiful life recognizes that this world and all in it belongs to God, and in such a world the worst thing that ever happens is never the last thing that happens.

A little girl was scheduled to recite some scripture verses for a children's day program in church. She had gone over and over one particular verse, but when she stood before the congregation her mouth went dry and her mind went blank. In the front pew her mother tried to calm her down by silently forming the opening words of the scripture verse with her lips, "I am the light of the world. . . . " The little girl relaxed, and she confidently began, "*My mother* is the light of the world. . . ."

That's not exactly how the verse goes, but it's not unscriptural. Jesus said he is the light of the world, but he said his disciples are the light of the world also (John 8:1; Matt 5:14). Such radiance is something of the beauty of the Lord in us.

I have some real problems with folks who are overly cautious, critical, negative about life. Faith may be risky, but the result is well worth the risk. Trusting others may be dangerous, but the worse danger is believing everyone is living just for himself or herself. Generosity may result in losses, but the greater loss is greed.

Bro. Dave Gardner used to say, "Tell me something you believe in; I have enough doubts of my own." I know enough about the dangers, the bad side of life. A lot of folks still think the world is going to the dogs, even if the dogs have had a long wait.

This world still belongs to God. God will have the last say. Whoever believes that, whoever knows that and encourages others to believe it, has about her or him a radiance that can light the way for others, a radiance characteristic of the beauty that goes clear to the bone.

Real beauty goes clear to the bone. And real beauty has about it a certain *wholeness*, a certain *harmony and balance*, and a certain *radiance*.

Have you looked in the mirror lately? Amen.[16]

"Examine Yourself First . . ."
A Lord's Supper Lesson

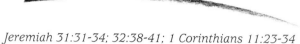

Jeremiah 31:31-34; 32:38-41; 1 Corinthians 11:23-34

> That's why you must examine the way you eat and drink. If you
> fail to understand that you are the body of the Lord, you will
> condemn yourselves by the way you eat and drink. . . .
>
> —1 Cor 11:28-29 CEV

Some time ago I was casting about in my library, not looking for
anything in particular, just trolling up and down the shelves, to
refresh my own mind about the Lord's Supper. I was probably
unconsciously hoping that what someone else said on the subject
would grab hold. And something did.

I was looking in my *Orthodox Study Bible*, among the pages of
the Corinthian letters, when I noticed a note about the Lord's
Supper. The commentator explained what the Lord's Supper
means to Christians. Then he intimated that Orthodox Christians
do it the right way, Roman Catholics almost do it the right way,
but Protestants rarely do it at all because Protestants don't really
understand it. . . . That's what he says. We don't understand the
grand, spiritual significance of this piece of worship called the
Eucharist or Holy Communion or the Lord's Supper.[17]

That Greek Orthodox commentator may be right. We may not
really understand the grand, spiritual, eternal significance of this
thing we call the Lord's Supper. I hope he is *not* altogether right. I
hope we understand better than we sometimes appear to understand. But if someone else gets the impression that we don't
really understand and appreciate the significance of the Lord's
Supper, perhaps we need at least to examine that.

Paul's advice to the Corinthians was good advice then, and it
still is: Before you come to the Lord's table, Paul said, "examine
yourselves." I propose you and I do just that, here and now,

before we get to the table. Then perhaps, just perhaps, we may remember who we are—the body of Christ, his church. Perhaps, just perhaps, we can remember and even understand.

Let us pray.

> When I survey the wondrous cross,
> On which the Prince of Glory died,
> My richest gain I count but loss,
> And pour contempt on all my pride.

Lord God, our Father, it is a humbling thing to be died for. Today at this table we remember that Jesus Christ, God's Son, our Lord, did exactly that for each one of us. Jesus went to his death knowing full well how often we would forget. Jesus went to the cross feeling the pain of the sins we were yet to commit, knowing that we would never really understand the depth and height, the length and breadth of God's love.

Lord God, let no pride in us keep us this morning from kneeling at the foot of the cross.

Melt the coldness of our hearts. Soften the stubbornness of our wills. As we take the bread and the cup, help us to enter into a new understanding of this grand mystery that unites the hearts and lives of Christians everywhere.

So may we feel God closer in a new and wonderful way, knowing that we shall never be alone again, since God who loved us and died for us is even now in spirit among us, as near as breath and as vital as the beating of our hearts. In the name and spirit of our Lord Jesus Christ, we pray. Amen.[18]

So then, you should each examine yourself first, and then eat the bread and drink from the cup. (1 Cor 11:28 TEV)

One December evening in 1975, Father Edward T. Cate—may his memory be a blessing—who was then the rector of St. James Episcopal Church in Livingston, Alabama, called to say he needed a deacon to help him celebrate the Eucharist, the Lord's Supper, at the Christmas Eve Mass. So I dressed out, including an alb, cape, and stole, and helped him serve the Lord's Supper to a full house at midnight on Christmas Eve. It became a regular thing after that, that the pastor of the First Baptist Church in Livingston helped celebrate the Lord's Supper at St. James Episcopal Church on certain holy days. I have good memories of those times, both serious and not-so-serious memories. But I especially remember something of Ed Cate's homily at one of those services. He said,

> Let us examine ourselves before we eat the bread and drink the cup. Let us remember that we are the body of Christ, and that by this act we do reaffirm for ourselves and for all the world that God is God and that we are God's people.

It was good advice when Paul said the same thing to the Corinthians. It is good advice now.

Why are we here? Why are we here in this particular place on this particular day? When you get behind all the temporary, incidental reasons why we are in church today, all the way back to basics, to what matters, the answer is, we are here because we are invited.

Long ago, God said He would make a new covenant with His people, "I will give them one heart and one way . . . an everlasting covenant," and God did just that. This is the "new covenant," Jesus said, the new way of understanding who God is, what God is doing, and what God wants for and from us.

You and I are invited. "Come unto me," Jesus said. Jesus still says that. Come to this table, eat this bread, drink from this cup, remember me, and remember who you are.

The real Host at this table is the Lord. He invites anyone who will to come. You and I are here because we are invited.

Are we worthy? Of course not. We are not worthy. How could we be? If we had a thousand years to learn and do the right thing, we could never be worthy. There is only one who is worthy here, and that is the Host at the head of the table. But that is enough. It is enough if you and I admit our unworthiness, and throw ourselves on God's mercy and grace. It is enough.

If you and I measure the very best thoughts and actions of our lives, we will come up short. But if we realize that it is not us but God's grace that saves us . . . that is enough. When you realize the only thing you can do to "earn" God's grace is just to accept it, then you're free to be and to do good—even when nobody knows it. When you realize nothing you can do is good enough to save yourself, then you're free to trust God, really trust God.[19]

The Lord's Supper is about remembering who we are, that we are the Body of Christ. Because some of the Corinthians had so soon forgotten, Paul wrote to them about the Lord's Supper. Chapter 11 of 1 Corinthians is not about the *how-to* but about the *what-for* of the Lord's Supper.

So I close my eyes and think about that, about feeling right not only toward God but toward . . . anyone, everyone.

Jesus said,

> So when you are offering your gift at the altar, if you remember that your brother or sister has something against you, leave your gift there before the altar and go; first be reconciled to your brother or sister, and then come and offer your gift. (Matt 5:23-24 NRSV)

Or we should also recall that Jesus taught us to pray like this:

> Our Father in heaven, ... forgive us our debts, as we also have forgiven our debtors. (Matt 6:9, 12 NRSV)

John later explained that

> Those who say, "I love God," and hate their brothers or sisters, are liars; for those who do not love a brother or sister whom they have seen, cannot love God whom they have not seen. (1 John 4:20 NRSV)

So I close my eyes and look inside myself and look around at those next to, in front of, and behind me. And I have to ask, Is it right between us? If the answer is Yes, then it is because I have begun to understand the Lord's Supper. If the answer is No, then I must needs go and do whatever I can to make it right. Otherwise, I eat this bread and drink this cup and bring my offering and claim to love God to no avail and to my shame and to my own judgment.

The Last Supper was really the First Supper, the first supper of a new understanding of the right kind of relationship between God and God's people. The Last Supper was a beginning. Now it is our turn. As the bread crumbles between my teeth and the cup washes over my tongue, I can remember the breaking of the body of our Lord and the spilling of the blood.

It was a breaking and a spilling that can heal and bring together and strengthen and encourage and give real life and hope.

It can, if we will. But we must examine ourselves first.

Then it will be our turn.

> Come to the table.
> You're invited.
> Come.
> Amen.[20]

The Holy Common
Another Lord's Supper Lesson

Luke 22:14-20

When it was time for supper, Jesus and the Twelve gathered round the table. Jesus said to them, "I have really wanted to share this Passover meal with you before I suffer [what is surely to come]—for, I tell you, I will not eat another Passover meal until Passover is fulfilled, until God's kingdom comes."

Then Jesus took a cup, gave thanks, and said, "Take this, and share it with each other—for, I tell you, I will not drink wine again until the kingdom of God comes."

Then Jesus took some bread, gave thanks, broke the bread, gave it to them, and said, "This is my body, which is being given for you. Take it and eat, in remembrance of me."

Then, when they all had eaten, Jesus again took the cup and said, "This cup represents the new covenant, confirmed by my own blood, which is being poured out for you."

— Luke 22:14-20 (my paraphrase)

Communion

His gospel sounds in every wind that sings,
His footprints linger where He never trod,
Because He took life's elemental things
And held them up to God.
So we recall Him: in a cattle stable,
In fishers' boats, beside a leper's bed;
And how He sat one fateful night at table
And blessed our daily bread.[21]

—William Gay

Jesus was a Jew. So were his family and his friends and the Twelve. At the time, the most important holy day of celebration for Jews was Pesach or Passover. It still is. Every year and all over the world, Jews still celebrate Passover as a special time of remembrance, remembrance of God's creation, salvation, and continuing watchcare.

In Jesus' time many Jews gathered in Jerusalem to celebrate Passover. That's why Jesus and his disciples were in Jerusalem on that fateful night we now call the night of the Last Supper, the night when Jesus began what Christians ever since have called the Lord's Supper or Communion or Eucharist (*Eucharist* simply means "gratitude" or "thanksgiving"). The Passover celebration centers around a meal, a Sabbath supper. The celebration still follows a rather standard pattern, probably much the same as it was in Jesus' time.

When everyone has gathered around the table, the head of the household prays an opening prayer, giving thanks and blessing the cup that is then passed around the table.

Then every person takes a sprig of bitter herb, dips it into salt water, and eats it. Eating the bitter herb recalls the bitterness of suffering prior to God's redemption. The salt may signify the sweat of slave labor—or the salt just helps make the bitter herb palatable. We may note that Jesus' reference to "the one who has dipped his hand in the bowl with me" (Matt 26:23) probably refers to this.

The head of the family takes a flat cake of unleavened bread, breaks it, and puts some aside. The youngest member of the family asks what all this means. The leader tells the story of the first Passover. They all sing two hymns, Psalms 113 and 114. Then they all join in eating the Passover meal of roast lamb.

Before the meal, everyone washes their hands. This was probably the point at which Jesus washed his disciples' feet (John 13:4-12). During the course of the meal, grace is said and bread is broken. And the bitter herbs are dipped in sauce and passed around by the leader. This is probably when Jesus gave "the sop" to Judas (John 13:26). It was at the close of the meal that Jesus instituted what we have come to call the Lord's Supper.

At the end of the supper, Jesus took one of the cakes of bread that had earlier been set aside, broke it, and passed it around the table. Finally, the Passover celebration ended with the singing of hymns or hallelujah psalms (Ps 115–118) and then the Great Hallel (Ps 136; *hallel* = "praise"). Such hymns are probably what Matthew refers to in Matthew 26:30. After the final breaking of bread and the singing of hymns, the final cup is passed around the table.

In outline, that is how Passover is celebrated, probably very much the same as in Jesus' day. Jesus' putting this remembrance celebration at the heart of the Passover explains what it means. Jesus has become the Passover lamb, offered up in sacrifice for the redemption of his people.

The cup, the wine, of course, represents his blood, his life, poured out for us. This outpouring ratifies the new covenant, a new agreement between God and God's people. When we accept that sacrifice for ourselves—which is symbolized by our eating the bread and drinking from the cup—and give our own lives into God's keeping, then God's salvation is for us too.

This is what we are to remember. Until Jesus comes again, we are to remember what God has done for us, that without God's grace and salvation we are enslaved to an existence that can end only in bitter, final death. But by God's grace we can throw off the chains of this body of death that enslave us and rise to new life. That is what we are to remember.

What does all this have to do with "the holy common"? Since the beginning of time the Jews have been remembering the most basic thing about life—God's creation and salvation and continuing care—by eating and drinking the most basic and common of things, bread and wine. When Jesus called upon his disciples to remember, he turned to the most basic and common things about life to use as symbols.

What is more common to life than the bread we eat and the drink we drink? Eat this; drink this, Jesus said. When you think about bread and drink, you have to think about the stuff that gives us life and keeps life going.

When Jesus told us to eat and drink and so remember, what did he want us to remember? He wanted us to remember the Cross, his death for us, surely. But bread and wine mean something more.

Jesus could have used almost anything to help us remember. He chose what is so common, but so vital—bread and wine.

Jesus wants us to remember also that just as the bread we eat and the drink we drink every day keeps us alive, so we must every day feed on Jesus to maintain our life in him.

So what is common is not really so common.

It is precious, priceless, holy, life itself.

Take this. Eat. Drink. Remember. Amen.

Looking for God
in All the Wrong Places

1 Corinthians 1:18-31

For the message about the cross is foolishness to those who are
perishing, but to us who are being saved it is the power of God.
—1 Corinthians 1:18 NRSV

Some of you will be sure I'm over the hill when I tell you my idea
of "country music" is Little Jimmy Dickens singing "Sleepin' at
the Foot of the Bed" or Eddy Arnold crooning "I'm a Plain Ol'
Country Boy." I can't identify with some of the stuff they call
"country music" these days. Once in a while, though, maybe on
the road somewhere, making a pit stop at a truck stop, somebody
with a fistful of quarters will punch up a song on the music box
that I can identify with—or that I think *somebody* can identify
with.

A few years ago I heard Mickey Gilley singing "Looking for
Love in All the Wrong Places." That might be the theme song for
a host of miserable folks these days—and we could wax eloquent
on the subject.

Professor Molly Marshall, back when she was teaching theology at the Southern Baptist Theological Seminary, said she heard
Mickey's song also, and she'd like to add a verse: "Looking for
God in All the Wrong Places." The Christians in Corinth, Molly
said, along with a host of other Christians closer to home, could
identify with that.

She's right. At least one of the problems for the Christians at
Corinth was that a lot of them were looking for God in a lot of the
wrong places. They didn't know it. And that's at least one reason
for Paul's letters to the Christians at Corinth.

Paul came to Corinth by way of Athens. In Athens he ran into some folks who, as Luke tells it, spent "all their time telling and hearing the latest new thing" (Acts 17:21 TEV), or, in the country version, they did "little else but discuss the latest fads and ideas" (CPV).

There was some of that among the Corinthians. They were faddish, always ready to jump on the latest bandwagon, but watching out for the next wagon to come along so they could jump on that one, too. They were impressed with what was different and showy and titillating—whatever gave them a thrill.

At Corinth—Paul noticed—their faddishness was apparent in their cliquishness. Paul denounced their "parties." There were at least three: those loyal to Paul, those partial to Apollos, and those claiming some relationship with Simon Peter.

Paul-the-church-planter got there first, before there was a church. Paul pitched a big tent down by the river, hauled in some sawdust, lined up some folding chairs, and held what we used to call a "protracted meeting." Some Corinthians were convinced by Paul's preaching, converted, and baptized—at least, Paul says, he baptized Crispus and Gaius. Anyway, there were enough to start a church. So Paul-the-church-planter moved on down the road to pitch his revival tent and start another church someplace else.

Now to keep a church going, it really helps to have a pastor. So Apollos from Alexandria came to Corinth and preached a trial sermon. Apollos was *some* preacher. Hardly any fathers dozed during his sermons. Very few mothers' attention wandered— excepting those who couldn't remember if they preset the oven. Even the young people quit writing notes long enough to listen to him. Of course, the church called him. And Apollos became the first full-time pastor of First Church, Corinth.

Sometime later—evidently—Simon Peter stopped off in Corinth, perhaps on his way to Rome. When Peter came by, they had a big meeting in the fellowship hall, around a big covered-dish supper. When everyone was full of fried chicken, green beans, corn muffins, and Luzianne tea, they leaned back and listened as Peter told them about Jesus. After all, Peter had *been there, done that,* and *had the T-shirt,* and he could tell them things about Jesus that no one else could.

Well, you know what happened. Three great preachers. Three almost overpowering personalities, each of whom made a tremendous impression on those young Christians at Corinth. Given the circumstances, it was inevitable that some were impressed by Paul, some by Apollos, some by Peter, some even by all three of them.

What did it mean to be a Christian to those Corinthians? Well, it depends on whom you ask. Some claimed Paul as their model. Rough, plain-spoken, no-nonsense Paul. After all, he was here first, and there wouldn't be a church if it weren't for Paul. "Besides, he baptized me," somebody said.

But someone overhearing all that Paul-talk says, "Let me tell you, Apollos is the one—especially after that rough-and-tumble Paul. Apollos is charming. He's educated, cultured, proper. (He has a full head of hair, too!) When he preaches he never uses rough language, and he gets all his declensions in the correct order and all his nouns and verbs in the right number. And he never, never points his finger."

But someone else jumps in and says, "*Nobody* can hold a candle to Peter. Peter was with Jesus. He was Jesus' number-one, right-hand man. Peter knows about the gospel firsthand. He's been there. . . . And didn't it just break your heart when he told about how he denied Jesus. Makes me humble just to think about that great old soul."

So, round and round it went. Paul. Apollos. Peter. . . .

Did you notice what Paul noticed? They were all impressed by the *messenger.* That's all they could talk about. Somehow, in all of that, the message and Jesus got lost . . . or forgotten . . . or ignored.

There was no dissension between Paul, Apollos, and Peter—at least not then. There's every indication that all three focused on and were faithful witnesses to the gospel. There's every indication that all three were in some measure effective witnesses at Corinth. But, to some extent they all three failed to communicate.

Paul partly blamed himself. But he also faulted the Corinthians.
. . . Some of them were *still* looking for God in the wrong places.

Paul and Apollos and Peter. All three of them were admirable
men. But the bottom line is, when it comes to what really matters, all three were just a finger pointing and a voice calling,
"Look to Jesus. He's the one to follow. The *only* one."

The problem at Corinth, however, went much deeper. More
than just personalities were involved. In his letter Paul brought up
the personality cliques—a symptom—as a way to get to the real
problem.

Paul diagnosed the Corinthians as being infected and infested
with the "wisdom of the world." The only cure, Paul said, is a
steady diet of the "wisdom of God."

Martin Luther had another name for both kinds of "wisdom":
he called the one a "theology of glory" and the other a "theology
of the cross."

Now this "wisdom of the world" or "theology of glory" with
which the Corinthians were infected is readily illustrated by band-
wagons and jumping on. It has to do with fads and faddishness.
Most of us understand the expression "jumping on the bandwagon." But probably few of us remember the origin of that
expression.

Years ago, before TV or even radio—or, as our children say,
"back when Daddy was alive"—when the circus came to town
there would be a big parade. The parade was (1) to let people
know the circus was in town and (2) to get people to come to the
circus—a kind of moving billboard or a live TV commercial.

So out front of the animals and clowns and other attractions
and distractions would be a big, high, and fabulously decorated
wagon drawn by teams of matched horses. It was a sight to see. It
was intended to be a sight to see.

But there was more. The smaller circuses might have just an
old theatre organ on the wagon pumping out catchy march tunes,
or even a calliope. But the bigger circuses had a brass band on
the wagon. It was a sight to see, and a sound to hear. And the
whole idea of the bandwagon was to impress people, to give
them a thrill, and to suggest that more thrills were to come.

The idea was to get people to "jump on" and join the parade, to come to the circus. Of course, the people did. The circus was a welcome, refreshing break in the everydayness of life. Something different, and showy, and titillating—something that gave them a momentary thrill.

There's nothing inherently wrong with that. A little circus is a good thing. What's wrong is to place more importance on it than it merits. What's very wrong is to think the thrill of the moment is the substance of eternity.

But that's exactly what happens to someone who follows the "wisdom of the world" or the "theology of glory." What's important to them is what is big and showy or smart and stylish or just different or thrilling or—to put it in some of the latest faddish terms—what feels good.

The ancient Corinthians had no monopoly on this disease. It's still with us. Churches who think buildings and budgets and programs and crowds and statistics are what matter. They're not. They *may be* the means to an end, but they are not why we are here. You know that.

Preachers who think the only service worth their time has to be accompanied by angelic choirs and bands of silver trumpets announcing their accomplishments to all the world. Thank God for some who are still going about doing good that many will never even hear about.

Church members who will lift no hand, raise no voice, open no pocketbook, unless attended by a permanent name plaque or at least a receipt that is legal tender on 15 April. Thank God there are still some around who care about what matters, and reach out and speak up and give themselves with no thought of crowns or stars.

Some Christians are infected by this disease in opposing ways. Some think the little they can do or say or give or be is unworthy. So they just crawl into themselves and don't do anything. Even this, though, is a symptom of the disease of the "theology of glory" that is caused by the universal virus called the "wisdom of the world."

The antidote, the cure, Paul said, is a steady diet of the "wisdom of God," the "theology of the cross." It's foolish—at least in the eyes of the world. You see, don't you?—that's why the Corinthians had focused on Jesus' exaltation—"Ain't God great!"—instead of the cross—"Ain't God foolish!"

The fact is, God *is in* the cross. And the reason so many, then and now, have missed God is because they are looking for God in all the wrong places.

I'm much impressed with some big churches—buildings, budgets, programs, all of it. There's nothing inherently wrong with that. The bigger, stronger, more effective, the better. We *can* miss God by looking for God there. But folks also can miss God in little churches with rundown buildings, puny budgets, and no programs at all. . . . It has to do with perspective.

Let me tell you a story. I could tell you a very similar story about a doctor I know in a little town in Virginia, or a chief-deputy sheriff in Alabama, or a grocery-store clerk in Southside Virginia. This story just happens to be about a preacher.

Many years ago a friend asked me to preach a summer revival in his church. He was pastor in a very small town in Alabama, had been for some time. He asked another preacher friend to lead the singing. So we went, and ended up swapping out on the preaching and the singing. As I recall, we ate a lot—fried chicken and ham and fried chicken and roast beef and fried chicken.

On the last Sunday afternoon, we were sitting on the front porch at the parsonage settling our fried chicken. Out of the blue, our singer-friend turned to our pastor-host and asked, "When are you going to get out of this one-horse town and this dead-end church?"

Our friend didn't answer for a while. . . . I kept my mouth shut.

Then he said (as best I can recall),

I may *die* here. These folks need somebody. Before I came here all they had was a parade of preachers who would breeze in for a while, put on a big show, and then go on to greener pastures. Like the circus, just passing through, and leaving behind a few memories and a lot of garbage. I don't know . . . I guess I just decided it was about time the children had a preacher around long enough to get to know him. And that it was time the old folks had someone to bury them who knew them well enough to know what their lives meant. . . .

That was the end of that conversation. . . .

I got too busy later on and haven't kept up very well with some of those old friends. But the last I heard he was still there, in that "one-horse town," in that "dead-end church." Still baptizing the children, scolding them when they're bad and encouraging them when they're good and hugging them no matter what; marrying them and baptizing their children; laughing with them and crying with them—just being there when they need him, and loving them. Hardly anybody else knows he's there. . . . But all the right folks know exactly where to find him.

The theology of the cross—God giving Himself to us, for us—you see, frees us to look for God in all the right places.

When you realize the only thing you can do to "earn" God's grace is just to accept it, then you're free to do good—even when nobody knows it.

When you realize nothing you can do is good enough to save yourself, then you're free to trust God, really trust God.

And in that freedom you can begin to find God in all the right places. Amen.[22]

What the Bible Says about Stuff

Genesis 45:16-20; Luke 17:22-37

[Pharaoh inviting Joseph's brothers to Egypt]: "Also regard not your stuff; for the good of all the land of Egypt is yours."
—Genesis 45:20 KJV ERV ASV

[Jesus, with regard to the end of the age]: "In that day, let him that shall be upon the housetop, and his stuff in the house, not come down to take it away; and let him also that is in the field, not return."
—Luke 17:31 KJV

You will be tempted to smile at the title—"What the Bible Says about Stuff." I hope you will resist the temptation. I am not trying to be funny. The Bible has a lot to say about stuff, some of it rather serious.

Yet some of the things the Bible says about stuff *are* intended to be humorous, even if darkly so. You will remember the story about Esau swapping his birthright, his future, for what we used to call "a mess of pottage," that is, for a bowl of bean soup.

Esau-the-outdoorsman had been out stomping around the woods all day, hunting. He came dragging in late in the evening, just in time to smell that the stew Jacob-the-homebody had been simmering all day long was right ready to dish up.

Esau was *very* hungry. The stew smelled *so* good. And here is where the NRSV translation is better than most: "Esau said to Jacob, 'Let me eat some of that red *stuff*, for I am famished!' " (Gen 25:30).

"Red stuff"—that's exactly what Genesis says—*red stuff*. A steaming mulligan stew with lots of big red beans, kidney beans maybe. "Give me some of that red stuff," Esau begged, "I am so hungry I could eat an ox!"

Of course, Jacob was crafty, and Esau was a little dumb—which is one of the main points of this ancient story—so Jacob took advantage of the situation and did some serious trading: he offered a big bowl of his stew, with a hunk of bread thrown in, in exchange, mind you, for the inheritance that would one day belong to Esau the firstborn. According to Walter Russell Bowie,

> So [Esau] made the deal. . . . he did not care enough for life's great possibilities to pay the price of present discipline. He must have what he wanted when he wanted it, and consequences could go hang. That was the critical weakness of Esau and that was his condemnation. *He lost tomorrow because he snatched so greedily at today.*[23]

"He lost tomorrow because he snatched so greedily at today." That is, as John S. Kselman put it, Esau was "thoughtless about the future in the face of present need . . . [and sold] his birthright to '*stuff* himself.' "[24]

Of course we can see the humor in this story—although it is dark humor—intending to point up how smart Jacob was and how foolish was Esau. And we can of course draw all kinds of lessons from this good story. There are many good lessons in this story about Esau and Jacob and some *red stuff*.

The main lesson it seems to me can be stated quite simply: "Esau squandered his very life because he was hungry for some stuff. Let us *not* go and do likewise."

Don't misread this as being against *stuff* as such. We need *some* stuff to make it in this world. Remember the story about Joseph and Egypt and Pharaoh?

When he learned Joseph's big family in Canaan was very hungry because of crop failures, Pharaoh told Joseph to take some of Pharaoh's own wagons and go to Canaan and bring the whole clan back to Egypt where there was bread and plenty.

Do you remember that? Do you remember what Pharaoh said to Joseph?

"Take the wagons," Pharaoh said. "Get all the children, all the mothers and fathers, and all the grandfathers and grandmothers. . . . Bring everyone. *And,*" Pharaoh added, "Don't bother about packing all your stuff and bringing it along; the best stuff in all Egypt is yours for the asking" (Gen 45:20 my paraphrase). Just leave your stuff in Canaan, Pharaoh said; we have all the stuff you will ever need in Egypt.

What kind of lessons would you draw from that tantalizing little story? The point is, after the family—all the children and their parents and grandparents—Pharaoh thought of the *stuff* Joseph's folks would need. Everybody needs *some* stuff to keep life and limb together and to make it in this world. It was thoughtful of Pharaoh to realize that. "Don't worry about your stuff," Pharaoh said; "we will supply all the stuff you need."

Then there's a really serious note in Luke 17, which reports some of Jesus' words about the coming of the Kingdom at the end of time.

Everyone will be eating and drinking, marrying and burying when it comes, Jesus said, just like it was in the days of Noah and in the time of Sodom and Gomorrah (Luke 17:26-28). That is, when the Kingdom comes, everything will seem normal, business as usual. It will happen suddenly, without warning, when you least expect it, Jesus said. When it does happen, you must be ready; right then, you must be ready.

Jesus emphasizes the point with a picture of a person resting in the cool of a summer evening on the patio. When it happens, Jesus said, that person must be ready to go; that person must not even go into the house to pick up his billfold or her purse or anything else. Jesus did not say billfold or purse or anything else; he said *stuff*.[25] You must forget about your stuff, Jesus said, and be ready to go.

"Disciples are ready for Jesus' return when they have renounced their attachment to possessions."[26] Let me rephrase that: We are fit for the Kingdom of God only when we have let go of our *stuff*.

There are many lessons to be learned from Jesus' words as reported in Luke 17. That is one of the most important. We are fit for the Kingdom only when we have let go our *stuff*.

The Bible has a lot to say about *stuff*. And this is serious stuff, and important. The end of the matter is this: Don't let your stuff get you down or hold you down or keep you from the Kingdom of God. No amount of stuff is worth it in the long run.

You know that. I know that. But, let's face it, we are sometimes as dumb as Esau when it comes to all the stuff we think we need right now. Yes, we are. Just as dumb. Because all that stuff still smells so good, and looks so good, and tastes so good, and feels so good, and . . . and we are all so hungry.

Almost forty years ago Milton Mayer gave a commencement address at a university graduation. Milton Mayer preached this commencement address, and then it was printed in the *Christian Century* (in 1958). It had an imaginative title: "Commencement Address." Regarding how easy it is for you and me to act dumb with regard to stuff, some of Mayer's words bear repeating. Remember, Mayer was speaking to graduating seniors at a university.

> Like your teachers and your parents before you [Mayer said], you will be told to do bad things in order to hold your job. . . . And if, in addition to holding your job, you want to be promoted, you will think of bad things to do on your own. And you will have good reasons for doing them. You will have [husbands and] wives (at least one apiece) and children to maintain. You will have a home and mortgage to enlarge. And life insurance, purchased against the certainty of death, dread of which in turn adds preciousness to staying alive at any price. And neighbors who are having their children's teeth straightened. Your dentists' bills alone will corrupt you.

Of course, Mayer was talking about the corrupting influence of *stuff*. He said that just getting and keeping and maintaining all the stuff we think we need, or even all the stuff we think our husbands or wives or children or grandchildren need, is enough to corrupt the devil himself. And who do we think we are to escape that terrible corruption.

At the end Mayer gets very biblical, as you would expect a good Jew to do, even one as acid-tongued as Milton Mayer. He concluded by saying that

What [we] need is what the psalmist knew he needed—a heart, not a head, of wisdom. . . . I do not know where you will get it. If I did, I would get it myself. . . . [It is] the gift of God. . . . I bespeak for you the gift of God.[27]

Yes, the Bible has a lot to say about *stuff*. Frankly, as the Rich Young Ruler and the bumper-crop farmer with the bigger barns and, extrabiblically, even Milton Mayer the acid-tongued Jewish journalist knew, the Bible wants us to realize that we are all in real danger of letting our stuff rule and ruin our lives. It is such a prevalent and pressing and real and especially human danger that it is frightening to face up to it.

Milton Mayer was right, you know. The only hope we have to keep our *stuff* from ruining us is the grace of God. I pray for you and for me that gift of grace. Amen.

Making the Most of Meanly Means

A Lesson about Perspective

Philippians 1:12-14; 19-21

> I want you to know, brethren, that what has happened to me has really served to advance the gospel.
>
> —Phil 1:12 RSV

Richard Lovelace (1618–1659), the seventeenth-century British Cavalier poet, was on two occasions a political prisoner in the Gatehouse at Westminster. During his first imprisonment he wrote a love poem to Althea. (That is probably why he called it "To Althea. From Prison.") In stanza 4 of that poem is found that well-worn phrase

> Stone walls do not a prison make,
> Nor iron bars a cage.

For "minds innocent and quiet," Lovelace explained, prison could become a secluded residence, a quiet retreat. Even prison, he concluded, could not, would not bind his spirit or his love. Because, he said,

> If I have freedom in my love
> And in my soul am free,
> Angels alone, that soar above,
> Enjoy such liberty.[28]

Fifty years later, Jeanne-Marie Bouvier de la Motte Guyon (1648–1717), the French mystic, always preaching and practicing Quietism, was herself a political prisoner at the Castle of Vincennes, Paris. That's when she composed her "Prisoner's Song," a poem in which she echoed the words of Lovelace.

> But though my wing is closely bound,
> My heart's at liberty;
> My prison walls cannot control
> The flight, the freedom of the soul.[29]

Then, more than a century after Lovelace, William Words-worth (1770–1850), that born-too-late poet, summed it all up:

> Stone walls a *prisoner* make, but *not a slave*.[30]

But long before Lovelace penned his love letter from prison, another prisoner wrote a love letter from another prison, the sentiments of which, knowingly or not, may well have been the inspiration for Lovelace, Guyon, Wordsworth, and company. That other prisoner was Paul. His love letter was to his brothers and sisters in Christ at Philippi. We call it the Letter to the Philippians. That ancient poetry may yet instruct and even inspire us also.

> Lest you be misinformed, I would have you know that my sufferings and restraints, far from being prejudicial to the gospel, have served to advance it. My bonds have borne witness to Christ, not only among the soldiers of the imperial guard, but in a far wider circle. Also, the same bonds, through my example, have inspired most of the brethren with boldness, so that trusting in the Lord they are more zealous than ever, and preach the word of God courageously and unflinchingly. . . .
>
> Isn't my joy reasonable? I know that all my present trials and sufferings will lead only to my salvation, and that in answer to your prayers the Spirit of Christ will be shed abundantly upon me. Thus will be fulfilled my earnest longing and hope, that I may never hang back through shame, but during this crisis, as always, may speak and act courageously; so that, whether I die as a martyr for His sake or live to labor in His service, He may be glorified in my body. Others may make choice between life and death. I gladly accept either alternative.
>
> —Phil 1:12-14, 19-21 RSV[31]

Have you ever visited someone in prison? I vividly remember my first visit to a real prison. I was a student at Howard College and student-pastor of two "half-time" churches. One of our church members had a nephew who—as he said—had "gotten in trouble." Real trouble. Would I go visit his nephew?, he asked.

The nephew was in what was then the maximum-security section of Kilby Prison in Montgomery. But because I was the closest he had to a pastor, they let me in to see him on a Sunday afternoon. He couldn't come to the visitor's room. I had to go to where he was.

That's the part I remember so vividly: following a guard down several short, narrow halls, stopping often before steel-clad doors that would not open until the one behind had clanged solidly shut. By the time we finally got to the prisoner's cell, I was a nervous wreck, longing for open spaces and fresh air.

Even now I remember that place—especially when I get the urge to complain about tight quarters or confining circumstances. I recall, for example, seeing my dormitory room at Howard College with new eyes when I returned to it after that visit to Kilby Prison. Before, my dorm room had seemed like a 2'x4' closet. Now it looked as big as all outdoors. Besides, I could go in or out anytime.

Since then I've been in all kinds of jails and prisons . . . as a visitor. And I always come away with that claustrophobic feeling. They say you never know what you can do until you have to do it. . . . They say. Well, I've had occasion to do what I couldn't do until I had to do it. But that boy on death row at Kilby Prison was shut up, cut off, closed in, incapacitated, the means for real life no longer available to him. I don't think I could survive being shut up and cut off and closed in like that.

There are all kinds of prisons, and all kinds of prisoners also. And neither stone walls nor iron bars are required.

In 1978, I went early to the Southern Baptist Convention, meeting in Atlanta, to attend the preconvention Pastor's Conference. A young man from Missouri named David Ring was there to give his testimony. (If you know about David, you know he is handicapped. He was born with cerebral palsy.)

After hearing David's testimony I couldn't get it out of my mind. When I got home I called and asked him to come to Livingston, Alabama, and speak to our people there. I especially wanted the students at Livingston University and our own teenagers to hear David's testimony. So, in January 1980, David came to Livingston. On Sunday morning he stood before the church.

> I'm here [he said] to brag on Jesus. . . . I may walk funny. I may talk funny. I may talk differently and slower than you. . . . But I get the job done! I've got a handicap. . . . I say, I've got a handicap. What's *your* problem? . . .

In a very real sense, David Ring is shut up, cut off, and closed in by his handicap. Nevertheless, the last I heard, he is still getting the job done, "bragging on Jesus."

There are all kinds of prisons, and prisoners too. I know a man who was *doubly* shut up, cut off, closed in.

In the first place, Paul was handicapped in some way. We tend to forget, but you can't really think of Paul apart from his "thorn in the flesh" (2 Cor 12:7). It was some kind of physical ailment or impairment that hindered him, a harassing infirmity he was always aware of and not too happy about either.

Don't look at me. I don't know what it was, either. Perhaps it was epilepsy, some say, or malaria, or eye troubles (see Gal 4:13-15). He could have been hard of hearing, some say. Maybe he just had a bad back that nagged at him and hurt from time to time. Maybe Paul had plantar warts. *Nobody* knows. But it *was* serious. Paul's description suggests it was painful, crippling, even humiliating. It was serious enough to mention prominently several times in his letters.

It was a hindrance, Paul said, but then it made him all the more aware of his utter dependence upon God. (Paul knew there are all kinds of prisons, and the prison of pride was one he wanted desperately to avoid.)

Besides, Paul said, his "thorn in the flesh" made others all the more aware that something or someone, something more than or other than this man with the "thorn in the flesh" was at work in

Paul. By himself alone, Paul with the "thorn in the flesh" could not accomplish what he did. . . . At least, that's how Paul saw it (2 Cor 12:7-9).

We know something of what Paul accomplished, "thorn in the flesh" and all. He burned up the roads all over the Roman Empire, racing from town to town as if eternity depended on it—which it did—preaching and teaching and baptizing, planting and organizing and building up churches.

Then they arrested him. They threw him in prison, "thorn in the flesh" and all. So he was doubly hindered, doubly shut up, cut off, closed in.

Can we really appreciate Paul's predicament? Already he was harassed, hampered, and hindered by some permanent physical impairment. Now he was locked up, shut in, cut off from his friends and family, from his work, from his world. His already meanly means had become yet more meanly. What would he do? . . . What could he do?

First of all, he managed somehow to put his predicament in perspective. It was very real. Painful. Humiliating. Debilitating. Paul makes no bones about that. He often speaks of the *suffering* he had to endure.

But, somehow, he managed to put it in its place. Paul somehow could see that his circumstances were just that—circumstances, and not the controlling factor in his life. He *was* a prisoner, but *not* a slave.

Paul told the Corinthians he thought God *allowed* him to keep his "thorn in the flesh" so his dependence on God would be even more apparent, and thus might even encourage others to let God work in their lives (2 Cor 12:8-10). Now he has the audacity to tell his friends at Philippi that his being in prison is—because of their prayers and by God's grace—going to turn out to be *something good*.

"I'm no prisoner of Rome," Paul declared. "I'm a prisoner of Jesus Christ! I may be shut up, cut off, and closed in, but I'm not finished. Not yet!" In the gloom of his prison, Paul's faith shown the brighter.

A man named Christian in John Bunyan's *Pilgrim's Progress* was shown a fire burning brightly at the foot of a wall—in spite of the fact that a man was continually throwing water on the fire. Christian's guide led him behind the wall where he showed him another man with what amounted to a hose in his hand attached to a full gasoline tanker: the more water thrown on the fire by the first man, the more fuel this one fed the flame.

When John Bunyan told that tale, he must have had Paul in mind. The more circumstances seemed bent on dampening Paul's faith, the brighter that flame burned within him. Paul's faith shown the brighter, you see, because he had hidden resources. Not just someone behind the wall, but right there in his prison with him. Paul was not alone in that prison. . . . Neither are we in ours.

So, Paul told the Philippians, "My circumstances have not hindered the gospel; rather, my being shut up in prison has really helped advance the gospel."

> In the first place [Paul said], now some people are preaching the gospel who need to be preaching it. I mean, *because of my circumstances*, they are telling others about Jesus. Oh, some of them are doing it for all the wrong reasons, because they're glad I'm locked up. Now they have their chance to be out front. But that's alright. They're still talking about Jesus. And they might not be, if I weren't shut up here.
>
> On the other hand, some folks are hearing the gospel who need to hear it, and they might not be if I weren't locked up in here. I mean, the whole palace guard eventually passes by here. And, when they do, I tell them about Jesus. They're listening, and they're hearing, because I'm locked up, shut up, closed in, and still telling them about the real freedom in the love of God to be found in Jesus Christ.

Paul was a preacher and recognized a good thing when he saw it. He had a captive audience. His guards were bound to that prison just as much as he was. And Paul made the most of the situation.

Nowhere does Paul's faith shine brighter than in those dark circumstances. He found a new "congregation." And because he was shut up in prison, some—who might not have done so otherwise—began telling others about the gospel.

Last but not least, from that prison Paul extended his witness to the ends of the earth: from his prison—as have others after him—he wrote letters that have influenced countless persons even until now. Charlotte Elliott, for example.

Charlotte Elliott (1789–1871) was a bedridden invalid for the last fifty years of her life. Yet, suffering and imprisoned by an invalid body, she devoted her best energies to doing good for others her whole life long. Among many other things, she wrote more than 150 hymn-poems. One night in 1834, she was unable to accompany her family to a big loyalty dinner at church (a new building was needed, and they were having a big fund-raising kickoff party). Charlotte lay awake all night, "tossed about with many a doubt," she said, and in that prison bed she wrote the hymn-poem that is one of the most familiar and beloved of all time, the seventh stanza of which is

> Just as I am—of that free love,
> "The breadth, length, depth, and height" to prove,
> Here for a season, then above—
> O lamb of God, I come! I come.

There are all kinds of prisons, and prisoners too. I've told you about some who were real prisoners of their circumstances—but not a slave among them.

Any one of us can be imprisoned, shut up, cut off, closed in by circumstances—most often not the stone-wall, iron-bar, or even "thorn-in-the-flesh" variety. Pride can imprison us. Or fear. And sometimes it is neither more nor less than greed or jealousy or hate or insecurity or inferiority or something else just as common to us all that locks us up and shuts us in this fragile frame.

How to be free, free to really live, free to enjoy God's grace in spite of any circumstance?

Charlotte Elliott, for one, found the answer: it is to come to God *just as I am*, with no excuses, no holding back, no qualifications—just as I am. That's what Paul did. That's what David Ring did. That's what Charlotte Elliott did.

What spiritual resources do Paul and David Ring and Charlotte Elliott have that we don't have? None. Absolutely none. They just got themselves up and gave themselves to God, just as they were, with what they had and with all they had.

What then shall you and I do with ourselves and with our meanly means? Amen.

How Long, O Lord? . . .

Habakkuk 1:1-4; 2:1-4

Our Lord, how long must I beg for your help before you listen?
—Habakkuk 1:2 CEV

The sentiments of the little book of Habakkuk are startling. Habakkuk has the unmitigated temerity to shake his fist in God's face, to accuse God of not doing God's job, of not living up to God's promises. "How long, O Lord?" Habakkuk asks. How long will God let things go on the way things are going? When is God going to do the right thing, and do away with the evil in the world? O Lord, how long?

Of course, it was a different world, a different set of circumstances. We live in a world far removed from Habakkuk's world. Yet Habakkuk asks the kind of questions human beings ask in every age and in all kinds of circumstances. Habakkuk gives us no simple answers. He offers some general ideas about life. And he gives some advice on how to hold on in times of confusion and difficulty. But Habakkuk does not relieve the frustrations we sometimes have. All he does is to set our perplexities in perspective.

Not that it helps very much, but life's always been this way. It may go on this way for yet a while.

Hear then the ancient yet very appropriate words of Habakkuk the prophet.

> I am Habakkuk the prophet. And this is the message that the Lord gave me. Our Lord, how long must I beg for your help before you listen? How long before you save us from all this violence? Why do you make me watch such terrible injustice? Why do you allow violence, lawlessness, crime, and cruelty to spread

everywhere? Laws cannot be enforced; justice is always the loser; criminals crowd out honest people and twist the laws around. (1:1-4 CEV)

While standing guard on the watchtower, I waited for the Lord's answer, before explaining the reason for my complaint. Then the Lord told me: "I will give you my message in the form of a vision. Write it clearly enough to be read at a glance. At the time I have decided, my words will come true. You can trust what I say about the future. It may take a long time, but keep on waiting—it will happen! I the Lord, refuse to accept anyone who is proud. Only those who live by faith are acceptable to me." (2:1-4 CEV)

Forgive us, O God, for our little ideas about the heart of God. Forgive us for our doubting suspicions and our confusion about how things ought to be.

Give us faithfulness. We say we have so little faith. Yet we have faith in each other. We have faith in checks and in banks, in automobiles and traffic lights, in unseen cooks in restaurants, in strangers who pilot the planes in which we fly around, in doctors with strange names and strange faces who doctor on us, in taxi drivers we have never seen before and may never see again. Forgive us our stupidity, that we have faith in people we don't even know and are so hesitant to trust God who knows us all the way through.

We are always looking for a complicated way through life. But you have plainly marked out a way for us. Help us to walk in it. So many of our troubles we bring on ourselves. How silly we are. Forgive us our silliness.

Then give us a faith we can deposit in the bank of your love, so we may receive the dividends of forgiveness and the interest of daily grace that you are so willing to give us.

We ask it all in the faithful name of our Lord Jesus Christ, whose faithfulness saves us and sustains us even in spite of our doubts. Amen.[32]

Habakkuk is one of those Old Testament prophets we really don't know much about. We are not even sure how to pronounce his funny name or what it means. Some scholars and other wiseacres want to pronounce it *Hah-bah-kook'*. But *Hah-back'-uk* is okay; and whether or not you remember to put the two Ks in the middle rather than on the end really doesn't matter very much.

We're not sure what his name means, but names are important in the Bible, so let me tell you what I think, and you can make up your own lesson. Habakkuk's name comes from a rare Semitic verb that means to *clasp* or *embrace*. In Genesis 29:13, when Jacob comes to visit his Uncle Laban, Laban *embraces* Jacob. The Hebrew text says he *habakkuked* him.

So, Habakkuk's name means *one who embraces another*. Habakkuk was a *hugger*. You know how important a hug is. And to have a hug, you have to have a hugger.

A few years ago, one of our children's teachers, Leontyne Espy, moved from the halls of the high school to the offices of the board of education. One day we saw Mrs. Espy in the grocery store, and my wife asked Mrs. Espy how she was getting on. Had she made the transition from the busy halls of the high school to the quiet offices of the board of education? Yes, she said, she was doing fine, but she missed the hugs. They don't hug much around the board of education offices, she said.

Have you hugged your children today? Or your mama and daddy? Or your wife, or your husband? Or your friend? Hugs are important. Huggers are important. Habakkuk was a hugger.

Martin Luther said that Habakkuk had the right name, because Habakkuk means "one who takes another to his arms." Luther went on to say that Habakkuk does this in his book: he comforts and quiets his people as one who takes a crying child into his arms, quieting the child, and telling the child that everything is going to be alright.

Habakkuk was able to take his people to his arms and tell them everything was going to be alright because God had taken Habakkuk to God's everlasting arms, quieted Habakkuk, and told him to wait and be patient, that everything *would* be alright. But before that, Habakkuk had to hold God at arm's length. Habakkuk questioned God! He accused God of not caring, of not doing what God was supposed to be doing. The passage we quoted above gets right to it.

> Our Lord, how long must I beg for your help before you listen?
> How long before you save us from all this violence? Why do you
> make me watch such terrible injustice? Why do you allow
> violence, lawlessness, crime, and cruelty to spread everywhere?
> Laws cannot be enforced; justice is always the loser; criminals
> crowd out honest people and twist the laws around. . . . (1:2-4
> CEV)

Does that sound familiar? Habakkuk was living during a time
when lawlessness, crime, cruelty, violence were everywhere. . . .

When is the last time you heard something like that?
Yesterday? In the newspaper this very morning?

The world hasn't changed much. We've come a long way, but
if you scratch the varnish off civilization, you find the same old
humanity: selfish, wicked, violent—just like it was in Habakkuk's
world.

And Habakkuk was fed up, just as some of us are. He had had
as much violence and crime and cruelty and lawlessness as he
could stand. So for a long time Habakkuk had been asking for
God's help.

Isn't that what we are supposed to do? To do the best we can
to make things right, but to keep on asking God for help because
we know that in the end only God can put things right?

That, after all, is what God is supposed to do. Put things right.
And bring in the Kingdom.

It is promised to us that if we pray, God will answer. It is
promised that if we ask, we will receive. In fact, Matthew reports
that Jesus himself said:

> Ask, and it will be given you; search, and you will find; knock,
> and the door will be opened for you. For everyone who asks
> receives, and everyone who searches finds, and for everyone
> who knocks, the door will be opened. (Matt 7:7-8 NRSV)

A long time before Jesus said that, Habakkuk believed it; at
least he wanted to believe it. But then something happened.

Habakkuk prayed and prayed and prayed. He prayed for God
to make things right, to clean up the mess this wicked world had

become. Things were all turned upside down in Habakkuk's world: bad things were happening to good people and—worse—good things were happening to bad people. It was a crazy situation—not unlike the kind of world you and I live in . . . or so it sometimes seems.

But it didn't happen. God did not make things right. Habakkuk kept on praying. But things kept on being the same. And worse.

Finally, Habakkuk had enough. So he had the gall, the temerity to call God to task. How long? he asked.

How long must I keep on crying to God for help when God does nothing? Nothing! I have asked. I have searched. I have knocked. I have done everything but kick the door in. Nothing! God has done nothing to punish the evildoers and to reward the good. How long will God keep on doing nothing . . . ?

I was barely a teenager the first time I pulled a Habakkuk. I had been taught all my life that prayer works: you ask God for help and, so long as you ask in the right way and ask for the right thing, God will answer. And I had been praying. Because Granny was dying.

We lived on a farm, close to the earth, close to the plants and animals. I knew about dying and death. I had seen it in the woods and fields and in the pig parlor and in the chicken yard and even in our family. I knew about death and dying. And I knew Granny was sick, very sick. I knew she was dying. So after sitting with Granny at her sickbed, Spot the Wonderdog and I would run down the hill to Black Creek, to Granny's favorite fishing hole, and I would pray out loud with no one to overhear but Spot and the fish.

I prayed, "Please God don't let my granny die. She is so young and so strong and so good, and I need her so much." Because Granny was my buddy. The closest boys my age lived miles away. So, most all the time, Granny was my buddy. She taught me how to pick cotton and milk a cow and bake a blackberry pie. She showed me how to fish and make ponebread and drink black coffee. She doctored my hurts and scolded me when I was bad and hugged me when I needed a hug—which was often. Granny was my best friend. Even today, after almost fifty years, I still sometimes miss my granny.

Don't let Granny die! I begged God.

Granny died. Years before her time. Which means of course years before I was ready for her to go. Granny died. And I ran out of the house, jumped the yard fence, ran across the road, climbed the field gate, and as hard as I could I ran to the back of the field to the edge of the dark woods that ran down to the spring, and I raised my little fists toward heaven and cried from deep down in my hurt, Why? Why did you let my granny die?

That wasn't the first time. It wasn't the last time. It may happen again.

I know my prayer was smaller than Habakkuk's. My concerns were smaller. I was smaller. But I can feel something of what Habakkuk must have felt. My whole world seemed out of joint, turned upside down: "truth forever on the scaffold, wrong forever on the throne." It may have been a little world, but it was *my* world. And God didn't fix it when I thought it needed fixing.

That's one reason Habakkuk is so important to us, to you and me. When it seems our heart will burst for hurting over our world that has somehow gone crazy, Habakkuk is there to let us know that we are not alone.

When God didn't answer your prayer, did you think you were the only one it ever happened to? No, Habakkuk says, it happened to me. It even happened to Jesus, except Jesus handled it better than most of us do.

That last night on his knees in the garden, Jesus prayed: If there is any way to get around this, any way to avoid this hurt. . . . But it happened anyway. The hurt. Even the dying.

And Jesus cried out about being forsaken. Don't soften that hard saying by explaining it away or letting someone explain it away for you: "My God, why have you forsaken me?!"

But let's get back to Habakkuk. "I waited for the Lord's answer," Habakkuk says (2:1).

Then the Lord told me: "I will give you my message in the form of a vision. Write it clearly enough to be read at a glance. At the time I have decided, my words will come true. You can trust what I say about the future. It may take a long time, but keep on waiting—it will happen!" (2:2-3 CEV)

It will happen, God told Habakkuk. What will happen? What Habakkuk was praying for.

> Things will be made right.
> Justice will prevail.
> Evildoers will be punished.
> Good people will be rewarded.
> The Kingdom of God will come.

But notice that key phrase "at the time I have decided . . . it will happen."

That's the rub, you see. God's time and our time are not the same. And God's view of the world and time and eternity is so much broader and higher and longer and bigger than our view could ever be. God sees the whole picture; we see only our little detail view.

God is at work, Habakkuk wants us to know, even when for lack of vision or understanding, perhaps because we are blinded by selfishness or by our own hard hurts, even when we cannot see it and have to struggle to believe it, God is at work in our world, and eventually, in God's own time, we will see and know. In the meantime, when faith falters for hurt or for lack of understanding, we can come round to the faithfulness of Habukkuk, which after all is what God requires—not understanding, but faithfulness.

Habakkuk finally said:

> Fig trees may no longer bloom, or vineyards produce grapes; olive trees may be fruitless, and harvest time a failure; sheep pens may be empty, and cattle stalls vacant—but I will celebrate because the Lord God saves me. The Lord gives me strength. He makes my feet as sure as those of a deer, and he helps me stand on the mountains. (3:17-19 CEV)

And we may add that

> In the darkest night of the year,
>   When the stars have all gone out,
> I know that courage is better than fear,
>   That faith is truer than doubt;
> And fierce though the [demons] may fight,
>   And long though the angels hide,
> I know that Truth and Right
>   Have the universe on their side;
> And that somewhere, beyond the stars,
>   Is a Love that is better than fate;
> When the night unlocks her bars
>   I shall see Him, and I will wait.
>   —Washington Gladden (1836–1918)

How long, O Lord? . . . In God's good time. And it will be in time and on time, whether we can see that or not. Can you believe that? Will you believe that? Even in the dark, or especially in the dark, it is better to walk with God by faith.

How long? Until we can celebrate with Habakkuk because the Lord God has saved, is saving, and will save us. Amen.

Three Wedding Homilies

You Are the Company You Keep
A Wedding Homily for Beth and Scott

Almost 500 years before Christ, the Greek playwright Euripides said something like, "You are known by the company you keep."[33] At least since then, mamas and daddys, teachers and preachers, and other keepers-of-our-souls-for-our-own-sake have been reminding us that we are in fact known by the company we keep.

It is true. Euripides was correct. At least he was partly correct. But there are more words than needed in "You are known by the company you keep." In truth, you *are* the company you keep.

Life has to do with relationships, keeping company with. With ourselves. With God. With our world. With each other. Here today we are recognizing and celebrating a specific relationship, one man and one woman who have chosen to keep company with each other, from now on and forever.

From now on, no one will be able to really know one of you without knowing the other. No one can rightly consider one of you without including the other. No one can actually understand one of you without some knowledge of the other. Because for better or worse, for richer or poorer, and all those other "fors," you two have chosen to keep company with each other.

All of us are here today to say to you that you have made the right choice. You have chosen to keep and are keeping the right company. All of us are here with you today to affirm and celebrate your choosing to keep each other's company. But I cannot resist the strong impulse to say to you both, just one more time, *Remember who you are.* You *are* the company you keep.

Scott, from now on you are not just Scott; you are Scott *and* Beth. That is your choice. It is a good choice.

Beth, from this day forward and always, you are not just Beth; you are Beth *and* Scott. You made that choice. You chose well.

Remember who you are.

Beth, no one came inquiring of you when it came to designating mother and father, sister and brother. But you *chose* Scott. You chose to delimit and define your very self by Scott. You did well.

Scott, when it came time to hand out mama and daddy and other assorted relations, no one asked for your input. But you *chose* Beth. You chose to fashion and form your very life within the parameters of a certain other whom you call Beth. You have chosen well.

Remember who you are.

Scott, you are the one person in all the world with whom Beth chooses to keep company. From now on and forever, Beth has chosen and chooses you.

Beth, you are the only person in all creation with whom Scott chooses to be in company. From the day of choosing forward, and for always, Scott has chosen and chooses you.

Remember who you are.

Scott and Beth, all the other company here present rejoices with you in the choices you have made. You have chosen well. Go then and—from now on and forever—remember who you are. Amen.

June 20, 1992
Macon, Georgia

Little Things Still Mean a Lot
A Wedding Homily for Rebecca and David

In the book of Ephesians, in the fifth chapter, the author says some important things about relationships. Let's read those few verses that have to do with relationships between neighbors and friends and others.

> Be careful then how you live, not as unwise people but as wise, making the most of the time, because the days are evil. So do not be foolish, but understand what the will of the Lord is. . . . be filled with the Spirit, as you sing psalms and hymns and

spiritual songs among yourselves, singing and making melody
to the Lord in your hearts, giving thanks to God the Father at all
times and for everything in the name of our Lord Jesus Christ.
(vv. 15-20 NRSV)

Then comes that big/little verse numbered 21.

> Be subject to one another out of reverence for Christ.

Being "subject to one another" does not mean that one of you
takes turns lording it over the other while the other takes turns
meekly submitting. It doesn't mean that at all. It does not mean
that one rules while the other cringes in submission.

It really is quite plain. It simply means . . . well, let me read
you a translation that is really true to the text.

> Out of respect for Christ, be courteously reverent to one
> another. (*The Message* 1993, 1996)

"Be courteously reverent to one another." That says it all.
When we use the word "reverence," we routinely use it in reference to God or to the things of God, such as God's house. We
need as well to be reverent toward each other.

To be reverent simply means to honor and respect. To honor
another for the person he or she is. To respect another for his or
her wants and wishes and opinions and even idiosyncrasies—all
those little things, good and even not so good, that make us the
very unique person each one of us is.

To respect. To pay attention. To give consideration. Be reverent toward each other. Pay attention to each other. That's all it
means. No more. No less.

But this reverence, this respect and consideration must be
tempered with courtesy. Which, in the simplest terms, means to
be sensitive and allow the other person his or her own space.

Every one of us needs some space, space to breathe, to
express ourselves, to live out our lives according to our own inner
light. To be courteous means to allow the other some space,

sometime even to be indulgent, sometime even in spite of what we think the other should be doing or saying or being.

"Be courteously reverent to one another." That's the only way it's going to work. No matter what you may think now, those vows you spoke will prove true: there will be *bad* times as well as *good* times. The trick is to work hard enough at courteous reverence toward each other to make the good times outweigh and outlast the bad. You can do it. But don't be fooled. It is not going to happen automatically. It is not going to happen without some genuine, serious effort from each one of you.

Both of you are muscle-tone conscious. You know you can't keep your muscles toned up without expending some effort. You have to work at it, not just once in a while when you feel like it but regularly, all the time.

The muscle tone in your marriage is going to require the same kind of regular effort, sometimes even strenuous effort, not just when you feel like it, but even, or perhaps especially, when you don't feel like it at all.

What's the alternative? Well, what happens if you become a couch potato? Your muscles atrophy, and your whole body suffers and eventually just literally falls apart. The same thing happens to marriages sometimes. It is so easy to forget or put off or just refuse to expend the effort to keep stretching those muscles of courteous reverence for each other. When that happens, relationships weaken and eventually just fall apart. Regular exercise is the key, both for your bodies and for your relationship.

Let me say just one thing more. Little things still matter. Benjamin Disraeli once said that "Little things affect little minds."[34] Like much else Disraeli said, he really missed the mark. Little things affect all kinds of minds. It is the little things that life is made of. I like the way Robert Browning said it:

> We find great things are made of little things,
> And little things go lessening till at last
> Comes God behind them.[35]

Being courteously reverent toward each other is a lot of little things all together, all the time, that eventually become great things like love that lasts . . . and then comes God behind all the great-little things.

On this great, grand, and glorious day, neither one of you will believe it—or you shouldn't—but I am going to tell you anyway, because it is true. One of the hardest things you two are going to have to learn is how to brush your teeth and wash your face at the same sink.

It really is the little things. Such as whether to squeeze the toothpaste from the middle or from the end. Like one of you leaving a wet washcloth right where the other wants to put an electric razor or a curling iron. Or whether to install the bathroom tissue so it rolls out over or under. . . . The little things.

I am not trying to be cute or funny. I am not even trying to shock you into listening. But I want you not just to listen but to hear. Little things mean a lot.

Just the way you speak to each other, not just when someone else is listening but when you are all alone. Not just what you say to each other but how you say it.

You say so much without ever opening your mouth. A husband or a wife can bring the other to tears just by slamming a door or throwing down a dishcloth. But a wife or a husband can bring joy and laughter to the other just by a touch at the right time and in the right kind of caring way.

You have to pay attention, and learn about and from each other. You have to learn when to say the right thing, and you have to learn when not to say the wrong thing.

And—regardless of what you may have heard or read or seen or somehow think—it is not easy. It requires attention, patience, and sometimes just plain hard work.

Nothing worthwhile is cheap. And lasting, rewarding, fulfilling love between a woman and a man doesn't just happen. You have to learn how and then work it out every day. Every little day. Every little hour. Every little minute.

But the end of the matter is, it really is worth it. And it really can and does keep getting better. So long as you keep on working at being courteously reverent or reverently courteous toward each other.

Great things really are made of little things, but the little things go lessening till at last—if you will let me revise Browning's words—comes lasting love, and home, and family. You have all the raw materials you require right here, in each other.

We all wish for you love and respect and courteous reverence for each other, for God's sake surely, but for your own sake and for ours as well.

March 22, 1997
Macon, Georgia

On Cutting Boards and Other Things
A Wedding Homily for Jackie and Ed

Most everyone has a favorite saying to call to mind when required. Was there ever a child who asked Mama or Daddy for some spending money who didn't, sooner or later, hear that grand old maxim, "Money doesn't grow on trees!" Everyone understands that.

Some such sayings hold a lot of truth. You have to be careful to apply them correctly. You wouldn't want to say "Look before you leap!" when "He who hesitates is lost" is required.

Then there's the old maxim mixup: "Keep your nose to the grindstone, your shoulder to the wheel, your hand on the tiller, your ear to the ground, your eye on the road . . . then try to work in that position."

My favorite saying is one my father taught me many years ago. Daddy was a carpenter, and when I was a boy he let me "help" him on certain jobs while he tried to teach me the art of "butchering wood."

At such times I noticed when he was sawing a piece of lumber he always cut on the *outside* of the line he had drawn. And he noticed that I tried to cut right on the line. That's what prompted him one day to tell me

> Measure twice, saw once,
>   and always cut outside the line.
> You can cut a board shorter,
>   but you can't cut it longer.

I was a father myself before I realized my daddy was trying to teach me, not just about cutting boards, but about life itself. In one's work, in the things you do and say, especially in relationships with others, "Measure twice, saw once, and always cut on the outside of the line" is a good rule to follow.

Some people seem to do just enough to meet the very lowest standards. There are lots of "short boards" around today because someone cut on the line or even inside the line. It is true in every area of life—perhaps especially in marriage.

You two have made a decision regarding the one and only with whom you want to share the rest of your life. All of you. All your life. One reason we are here today is to share with you the grand and fearful joy of that decision, to bless you in that decision, and to add our own hope to yours that it is indeed the right thing to do.

It is the right thing to do. You have made the right decision.

But this is not the end of anything. This is the beginning of your relationship as husband and wife. Now begins the best part: the working out of that relationship in real life.

"Before God and this company" you have affirmed your decision to share the rest of your lives as one. And you have reaffirmed that decision in the vows and pledges you have spoken and with the rings you have given and received. You have measured and remeasured your decision. You have drawn a line for everyone to see.

Don't fudge on that line. Cut outside the line.

Do for each other more than you have to do to get by. Expect from each other and from yourselves more than just "average" or "normal." There are lots of *average* and *normal* marriages out there in which normal wives and average husbands are slowly starving to death for lack of enough affection or caring or forgiveness or encouragement or hope or love.

Give more than you think you have to give. Marriage is not a 50-50 arrangement. It is a 100-100 relationship—200 percent from each of you.

When I was a boy, we often had "dinner on the ground" at church. Everyone would bring a truckful of food and tea and lemonade. The long wooden tables out under the oak trees would be almost swaybacked with the groceries stacked wall to wall at lunchtime. We would eat and drink and talk and laugh until the tea began to run out and the lemonade bucket went dry. But it seemed to me we hardly ever made a dent in the food. It was like the loaves and fishes when Jesus fed the crowds: everything seemed to multiply in defense of the ravenous appetites of the crowd.

I never wondered about such things. I simply asked my mother, "Why do people bring more food than anybody can eat and then haul home almost as much food as they brought?" "Because," she said, "it is better to have too much than too little. Better to take food home than someone not get enough at dinnertime. Besides, leftovers means supper is already cooked."

Don't worry about doing too much for each other. Don't fret over giving more than your share. You can't love or forgive or care or give more than enough. Besides, if there is some left over, it is like money in the bank to use when you need it. . . . And you will need it. Yes, you will.

It is not just an old saying that works well with cutting boards and other things. It is true of all of life. It is especially true—most everything is especially true—of husband-wife relationships, the most special relationship of all.

> Measure twice, saw once,
>   and always cut outside the line.
> You can cut a board shorter,
>   but you can't cut it longer.

June 7, 1997
Birmingham, Alabama

Notes

[1]Beth, Becca, and Eddie, at that time ages eight, six, and three. It was Father's Day, not Christmas. But it was very like Christmas.

[2]That is, "they" say it since Margaret Wolfe Hungerford (1855–1897) wrote "Beauty is in the eye of the beholder" in her *Molly Brown* (1878), a "translation," I suspect, of David Hume's (1711–1776) "Beauty in things exists in the mind which contemplates them" (in his essay "Of Tragedy").

[3]I cannot cite this in publication. I heard it from G. Avery Lee, who says he heard it in a Fosdick sermon at John D. Rockefeller's church (Riverside, New York City) sometime, way back when.

[4]Hester H. Cholmondeley, "Betrayal," in *Masterpieces of Religious Verse*, ed. James D. Morrison (New York: Harper & Brothers, 1948) 302.

[5]As remarked upon by James D. Smart in *The Quiet Revolution: The Radical Impact of Jesus on the Men of His Time* (Philadelphia: Westminster Press, 1969) 104-105.

[6]Edmon L. Rowell, Jr., *Apostles. Jesus' Special Helpers*, illustrated by James Padgett, BibLearn Series (Nashville: Broadman Press, 1979).

[7]Ray S. Anderson, *The Gospel according to Judas* (Colorado Springs CO: Helmers & Howard, 1991) vii, 1.

[8]Ibid., 152-53, 154-55.

[9]Isaac Bashevis Singer, "Isaac Bashevis Singer's Universe," *New York Times Magazine*, 3 December 1978.

[10]E. C. Hoskyns, *The Fourth Gospel*, 2nd ed., ed. F. N. Davey (London: Faber & Faber, 1947) 552.

[11]*The Gospel according to John*, 2 vols., Anchor Bible 29, 29A (New York: Doubleday, 1966, 1970) 2:1096.

[12]Lemuel = "devoted/belonging to God," only in the inscription to Prov 31 (v. 1 ETT) and in verse 4. Massa was the seventh son of Ishmael, and the eponymous ancestor of a North Arabian tribe (Gen 25:14; 1 Chron 1:30). (A people of Mas'a/Mas'ai are also mentioned by Tiglath-pileser III, in connection with inhabitants of Lema [Gen 25:15]. *Ancient Near Eastern Texts Relating to the Old Testament* [1950, 1955] 283.) The Heb *massa* can be rendered "burden/oracle," and is often used of prophetic oracles (Isa 13:1; Nahum 1:1; Hab 1:1; etc.). So NRSV renders the inscription as "The words of King Lemuel. An *oracle* that his mother taught him." NRSV prevaricates. *Massa* in prophetic use has an ominous sense, suggesting impending doom or God's judgment. Such is not present here. *Massa* at Prov 30:1 and 31:1 is best translated as "Massaite": at 31:1 as either "Lemuel, a king of Massa" or "King Lemuel of Massa." What does it matter? The words are true still.

[13]"In Hebrew this poem is an alphabetic acrostic: that is, each line begins with a successive letter of the alphabet. (Key v. 30 is penultimate—sin/shin—beginning with sheqer, "deceitful, deceptive.") Far from being mere chattel of the husband, the Hebrew wife appears as the responsible head of the household (cf. 11:16, 22; 12:4; 18:22; 21:9, 19). She provides for food and clothing (vv. 13-15, 19, 21-22), purchases property (31:16), engages in trade (vv. 18, 24), and exercises charity (vs. 20). Physical beauty is a matter of indifference (vs. 30); what is important is intelligence, kindness (vv. 25-26), industry (vv. 15, 17, 27), and above all a religious spirit (v. 30)." Robert C. Dentan, "Proverbs," *Interpreter's One-Volume Commentary on the Bible* (Nashville: Abingdon Press, 1971) 319b.

[14]During the second century, the Shema was enlarged to include Deut 11:13-21 and Num 15:37-41.

[15]"Cumbered" KJV, ASV; "worried" AT, NTNT (Moffatt), PME (Phillips), NTLP (Williams), NTLT (Beck); "busy" NCE; "burdened" NAB; "rushing around" CPV; "upset" TEV; "distracted" RSV, NRSV, NEB, REB, NASV, NIV, NKJV. *Perispao/perispaomai* here is a figurative extension of the basic meaning "to be drawn away/off from around," "to be so overburdened by various distractions as to be worried and anxious" (*Greek-English Lexicon* [UBS, 1988] 1:314b). The basic meaning is instructive, as Jesus' response in verses 41-42 makes clear: by her too-much attention to too-many things, Martha was "drawn away from" what was really important.

[16]The basic plan (title and outline) and even one illustration of this sermon follows a sermon by Raymond E. Balcomb, "The Beauty That Is Not Vain," in *The Minister's Manual (Doran's)* 39 (1964) (New York: Harper & Row, 1963) 154-56.

[17]See the "theological note" on "The Eucharist," in *The Orthodox Study Bible. New Testament and Psalms. New King James Version* (Nashville: Thomas Nelson, 1993) 392 (at 1 Cor 11).

[18]After a prayer by Peter Marshall, "Worldwide Communion Sunday," in *The Prayers of Peter Marshall*, ed. Catherine Marshall (New York: McGraw-Hill Book Co., 1954) 82.

[19]From a sermon "Looking for God in All the Wrong Places," below.

[20]"Examine yourself first" was suggested by Ed Cate's homily and by an outline by Glenn H. Asquith, "Examination," in the *Christian Herald* (1958) as reprinted in *The Minister's Manual* 38 (1963) (New York: Harper & Row, 1962) 37-38.

[21]William Gay's poem appeared among the "Communion Poems" in *The Minister's Manual (Doran's)* (1963), ed. M. K. W. Heicher (New York and Evanston: Harper & Row, 1962) 45-46. The emphasis is mine.

[22]The idea of applying Mickey Gilley's song to the situation at Corinth is Molly Marshall's. I read about it in her article on "1 Corinthians 1:18-31," *Review and Expositor* 85 (Fall 1988): 683-86.

[23]Walter Russell Bowie, "The Book of Genesis. Exposition," *The Interpreter's Bible*, vol. 1 (New York and Nashville: Abingdon Press, 1952) 667a; emphasis mine.

[24]John S. Kselman, "Genesis," *Harper's Bible Commentary*, ed. James L. Mays et al. (San Francisco: Harper & Row, 1988) 102a; emphasis mine. "Feed me" (KJV) or some variation thereof, as in most English versions, is better translated "*stuff* me": the Hebrew verb normally is used with reference to "stuffing" cattle with food, in preparation of course for slaughter.

[25]At least the KJV rightly renders the term as *stuff*. Perhaps more polite, but probably less accurate, versions variously render it as *goods, belongings, possessions*, and so forth.

[26]Robert J. Karris, "The Gospel according to Luke," *The New Jerome Biblical Commentary*, ed. Raymond E. Brown, Joseph A. Fitzmyer, and Roland E. Murphy (Englewood Cliffs NJ: Prentice Hall, 1990) 710a.

[27]Milton Mayer, "Commencement Address," the *Christian Century* (14 May 1958), as reprinted in *What Can a Man Do?* (Chicago: University of Chicago Press, 1964) 147-53.

[28]This and the two lines above are from Lovelace's "To Althea, from Prison," stanza 4, as in *The Oxford Book of English Verse*, ed. Arthur Quiller-Couch, 2nd ed. (New York and Toronto: Oxford University Press, 1939; 11900) 384-85 (#357).

[29]From "A Prisoner's Song, Castle of Vincennes, France" (1695–1703), not in my library, so for citation I resort to "Bartlett's": *Familiar Quotations. A collection of passages, phrases, and proverbs traced to their sources in ancient and modern literature*, by John Bartlett, 15th and 125th anniversary ed. (Boston and Toronto: Little, Brown and Co., Inc., 1980; 1st ed. 1855) 296n.3 (the note is to Lovelace, quoted above).

[30]From "Humanity," one of Wordsworth's more obscure pieces, also not in my library, so I must again resort to Bartlett's to cite, again from a note to Lovelace: Bartlett's, 296n.2.

[31]This translation (or, rather, paraphrase) follows that of Joseph Barber Lightfoot (1828—1889) in his *St. Paul's Epistle to the Philippians. A Revised Text with Introduction, Notes, and Dissertations* (London: MacMillan and Co., 1913 repr. of 12th ed. [1896]; 1st ed., 1868) 87, 90-92.

[32]Adapted from a prayer by Peter Marshall, "For More Faith," in *The Prayers of Peter Marshall*, ed. Catherine Marshall (New York: McGraw-Hill Book Co., 1954) 18.

[33]Euripides (485–406 B.C.E.): "Every man is like the company he is wont to keep." Fragment 809 from his no-longer-extant play *Phoenix*, as quoted by Aristophenes (ca. 450–388 B.C.E.) in *Thesmophoriazusae* (411, a satire on Euripides).

[34]Benjamin Disraeli (1804–1881), *Sybil* 3.2.

[35]Robert Browning (1812–1889), *Mr. Sludge*, "The Medium," line 1112.